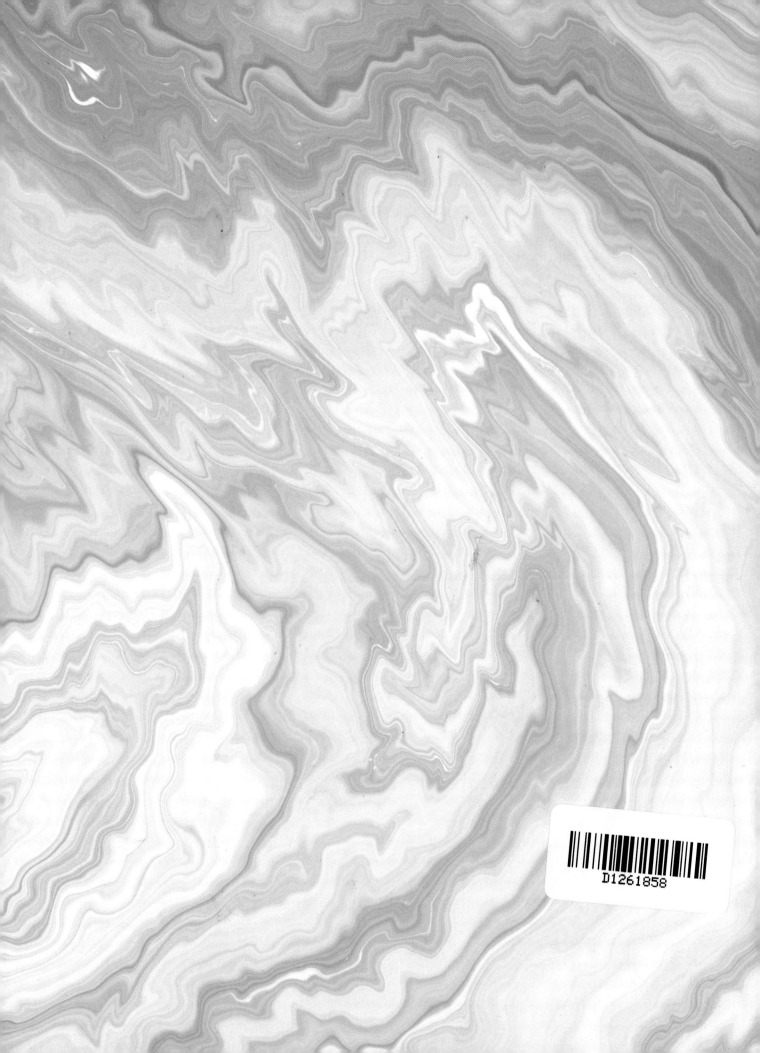

Tiffin Modern:
Mid-Century Art Glass

Ruth Hemminger,
Ed Goshe, & Leslie Piña

4880 Lower Valley Road, Atglen, PA 19310 USA

Credits

When the five of us — Ed Goshe, Ruth and Lyman Hemminger, and Leslie and Ramón Piña — gathered in Tiffin, Ohio to photograph the glass for *Tiffin Glass 1914-1940*, we realized that at least another book would be needed if we were to do any justice to the topic. When the time came, rather than use the photos of modern Tiffin glass we had previously taken, we decided to start a brand new project. So the same group of five gathered in Tiffin and photographed everything again, plus many newly-acquired and discovered pieces.

Naturally, the project became bigger than we had expected, and we would like to extend our thanks to the many people who contributed by generously lending examples of this beautiful glass (some, more than once) and/or by providing other material and information: Mike Bridinger, Dale and Eunice Cover, Ginny and Dick Distel, Gary C. and Jan L. Dundore, Phil and Rayella Engle, Ann Forrest, Madolyn Nichols Key, Robert A. and Donna L. Overholt, Paul and Nellie's Antiques in Tiffin, Bill Reyer, Crystal Rohrbacher, the Seneca County Museum in Tiffin, Pat and Joe Shumway, and a close friend who wishes to remain anonymous.

We are also grateful to those who helped us at libraries and other public institutions, especially: the Cleveland Public Library, Cleveland, Ohio for bringing mountains of journals out of storage; the Center for Archival Collections, Bowling Green State University, Bowling Green, Ohio; the Rakow Library of the Corning Glass Center, Corning, New York; and the Seneca County Museum, Tiffin, Ohio.

A very special thanks to John Bing for his good advice, dedicated assistance with the manuscript... and gourmet pancakes. Again, thanks to Doug Congdon-Martin and the staff at Schiffer Publishing and especially to Peter Schiffer for his exemplary attitude, encouragement, and friendship.

Hemminger, Ruth.
    Tiffin modern : mid-century art glass / Ruth Hemminger, Ed Goshe,& Leslie Piña.
        p.   cm.
    Includes bibliographical references and index.
    ISBN 0-7643-0320-1
    1. Tiffin Glass Company--Catalogs. 2. Art glass--Ohio--Tiffin--History--20th century--Catalogs. I. Goshe, Ed. II. Piña, Leslie A., 1947- . III. Title.
NK5198.T53A4   1997
748.29171'24--dc21   97-11399
                                          CIP

Published by Schiffer Publishing Ltd.
4880 Lower Valley Road
Atglen, PA 19310
Phone: (610) 593-1777; Fax: (610) 593-2002
E-mail:Schifferbk@aol.com
Please write for a free catalog.
This book may be purchased from the publisher.
Please include $2.95 for shipping.
Try your bookstore first.

We are interested in hearing from authors with book ideas on related subjects.

ISBN: 0-7643-0320-1
Printed in Hong Kong

Contents

Preface

The Other Fifties Glass

Mid-century—the 1940s, 50s, and 60s—seems too recent to be called a period in the history of decorative arts, but researchers and collectors have discovered that modernism did not end with the early styles such as Art Deco, with its many facets. The years just before and after the Second World War saw a phase of modernism in which free form replaced machine-age symmetry, hard angular edges dissolved into organic amoeboid shapes, and whimsical playful themes entered the design vocabulary.

Labels like "fifties glass" or "mid-century glass" do not refer to all categories of glass production circa the 1950s. In fact, a good deal, perhaps the majority of glass produced internationally during those years, was neither innovative nor modern. The mainstay of many glass companies, especially in America, was historic tried-and-true styles or mass-produced utilitarian wares with little or no style. The category known as "fifties glass" covers specifically the "designer" glass made by individuals or teams working in studio departments of larger glass factories or in factories organized in a similar manner. Though international, this designer-driven movement was centered in two specific geographic areas: Scandinavia and Italy, or even more specifically, the island of Murano off Venice.

As with any field, from architecture to fashion, the simpler the design, the fewer are the opportunities to disguise mistakes. Good unembellished form challenges both designers and artisans. While ornament, trim, and pattern add interest, they also provide wider margins for error or conceal imperfections. In order to be effective, simple designs must be perfectly proportioned and executed. Colorless or pastel-colored glass must be flawlessly clear; simple minimalist shapes must be graceful and true to the medium—reminders that the glass was once a hot and syrupy liquid.

Scandinavian glassmakers have continually accepted the challenge of producing simply elegant forms, and they enjoyed international acclaim for reaching new heights in glassmaking at mid-century. With exceptions such as the bold, colorful, overall pattern of Sven Palmqvist's Ravenna technique, Scandinavian color has been used with restraint. Its thick walls and sensuous, perfectly-executed forms define the style, while internal decoration, often extraordinary in its own right, is subordinate. The glass is, therefore, rarely confused with Italian fifties glass, which depends so much on vibrant colors and complexity of decorative patterns for its success. Where Murano artists explored and perfected colorful techniques using filigree, canes, mosaic, and metallic powders, Swedish artists invented less flamboyant Graal, Ariel, Kraka, and Ravenna, and in Finland and Denmark color was more often spare or absent.

Scandinavian fifties glass at its best ranges from cool, icy, minimalist forms to modernist paintings within glass, and examples fitting this description are naturally assumed to be from one of the Scandinavian countries. But in 1940 there was a fortuitous turn of events, when the Tiffin Glass Co. made the decision to introduce a line of "Swedish Modern" glass that would soon occupy a good deal of the company's creative and technical resources. Swedish designers and glassmakers carried the craft and the look of mid-century Swedish glass to a versatile, yet largely traditional, company in Ohio. Rather than copy modern Swedish glass, these talented individuals brought the technical skill and vision to create a new expression of the mid-century style, characterized by intriguing thick-walled shapes in colors ranging from a delicate pastel lavender named Twilight to brilliant Ruby red and Persimmon. Today, Tiffin Modern, especially pieces from the Empress line and its look-alikes, with spectacular, uninhibited free form vessels, are among the most collectible and the most extraordinary of any Tiffin glass. Not European, but American glass of original design and superb quality, Tiffin Modern is the other fifties glass.

Leslie Piña,
January, 1997

Introduction

Ruth Hemminger

The Tiffin Glass Company entered the glassmaking industry in Tiffin, Ohio, in 1889. Beginning as a pressed tumbler operation, the company continued to produce fine quality glassware for worldwide markets for over nine decades. The ability to manufacture a wide diversity of products enabled Tiffin to retain a prominent position in this highly competitive field until the final days of production in 1980.

The original factory was built by the A.J. Beatty & Sons, Inc., glassmakers from Steubenville, Ohio, who were attracted to Tiffin by the promise of free natural gas for five years. Production of the first tumblers took place on August 15, 1889. Capacity of this new factory was reported to be 500,000 tumblers per week. The Beatty factory merged with the United States Glass Company on January 1, 1892, and the Tiffin works was subsequently known as Factory R, one of nineteen factories owned by the huge U.S. Glass conglomerate.

Pressed tableware gradually lost favor with the American homemaker, and by 1914 blown stemware and cut crystal patterns were in demand. Tiffin responded with beautiful cuttings and acid-etched designs which they applied to stemware in Crystal, as well as Rose Pink, Reflex Green, Amber and Mandarin colors. Sales soared and Tiffin's position as a leader in the glass industry was secured. Many of these early lines have retained their popularity to the present time.

In the 1920s Tiffin began the production of satin glass. The satin appearance was achieved by immersing the glass object in an acid bath, resulting in a silky smooth finish that resembled satin cloth. Tiffin's Black Satin was recognized throughout the industry as the finest satin glass made, a distinction that it still enjoys today. Other glass companies offered this new ware, but none could compare to the superior quality of that produced at Factory R. In addition to Black, several soft pastel hues were offered in a satin finish, and satin ware remained popular throughout the thirties.

The Great Depression forced the closure of many of the original U.S. Glass factories. Factory R at Tiffin survived, and in 1937 the main office of the U.S. Glass Company was moved from Pittsburgh, Pennsylvania to Tiffin, Ohio. Major changes soon began to take place under the direction of President C.W. Carlson. An attorney and an astute businessman, Mr. Carlson was determined to produce the finest glassware possible. Strict quality control of all raw materials was initiated, and precise handling procedures were undertaken to ensure that the Tiffin name would be associated with quality and excellence.

Mr. Carlson was constantly searching for new ideas, and Tiffin's skilled workers were encouraged to experiment in order to create unusual and unique designs. Tiffin was fortunate to have some of the finest glassworkers in the world in their employ. Several Swedish workers had brought their families to Tiffin years earlier, and these skilled craftsmen were among those responsible for developing many of the new techniques implemented at the Tiffin plant. The names of Theller, Widegren, Wahl, LaMaire, Meier, Wolf, Mitchell, Fleming and Hoover are familiar to Tiffin collectors; these were only a few of the accomplished artists who propelled Tiffin to the top of the glassmaking business in the 1940-1950 era.

Among the innovative lines developed during the "Carlson Era" were Tiffin's Swedish Optic line (later named Tiffin Optic), introduced in 1940, and the superb sand carvings which were applied to beautiful hand-fashioned vases and bowls. Graceful new shapes and brilliant, bold colors highlighted the creative efforts of the skilled Tiffin artists. The colors of Copen Blue, Killarney, Wistaria and Twilight were introduced during this period.

In 1947 Tiffin presented another line that gained the attention and approval of glass enthusiasts everywhere. Perhaps the most beautiful of all the Tiffin stems, the Cellini line was also the most fragile and the most difficult line to produce. Requiring a minimum of sixteen workers, these delicate open work creations are truly works of art that only the most highly skilled workers were capable of producing. Tiffin's Cellini is art glass at its finest. During this same period, Tiffin applied numerous decorative treatments to a variety of Modern shapes in an effort to remain a leader in the competitive glass industry. Air twist stems with colored streamers were offered, gold encrustations were applied to vases, bowls and stemware, and a line of Mica ware was developed. A green "ribbon" decoration was applied to Crystal to create an unusual line, and a group of "Scallop Edge" bowls were produced in Twilight.

Tiffin's Empress line, introduced in 1959, was in sharp contrast to previous Tiffin designs. The large free form cased flower arrangers, bowls, vases and ash trays were made in various two-color combinations in many unusual shapes. Some pieces resemble the Modern designs employed by other glass manufacturers of that same era; obviously, all were competing for the same markets. The massive sizes of several of the Empress pieces are impressive; some measure over twenty inches. It is remarkable that the workers were able to control the large masses of molten glass required to create these beautiful objects. The most striking Empress pieces are those produced in Ruby and Crystal; the most elusive are the Twilight and Green combinations. All Empress pieces are wonderful examples of Tiffin Glass artistry.

While much interest was focused on Tiffin's Modern lines during Mr. Carlson's tenure as president, the production of fine quality crystal stemware continued at the Tiffin factory. Hundreds of cut patterns were produced for major department stores all over the United States and several other countries. A gold sticker was used for identification purposes. The Tiffin mark was applied by use of an acid stamp for a brief period only in the later years.

In 1955 the Duncan and Miller Glass Company of Washington, Pennsylvania, discontinued operations and many of their molds were purchased for use by Tiffin Glass. Several Duncan pressed patterns were reproduced by Tiffin in Crystal and other Tiffin colors. Included were Duncan's Canterbury, Hobnail, Early American Sandwich, Teardrop, Pall Mall, Patio, Murano and American Way patterns.

The retirement of Mr. Carlson in 1959 marked the end of an exciting era in the history of Tiffin Glass. Some of Tiffin's finest creations were developed and produced under his leadership. Mr. Carlson's goal of excellence was achieved through his genius and through the talents of the skilled Tiffin workers whom he proudly and rightfully named the "Tiffin Glassmasters." The sale of the business to an investment firm in New York took place soon after Mr. Carlson's retirement, and, in three years, the financial situation had deteriorated to the point of bankruptcy. The Tiffin factory was closed for several months, but reopened in 1963 as the Tiffin Art Glass Company. Purchased by C.W. Carlson Jr. and three former employees, the Tiffin factory resumed business with Mr. Carlson Sr., rejoining the organization. In 1964 the assets of the T.G. Hawkes Company of Corning, New York were acquired by the Tiffin Art Glass company. Two new colors, Citron Green and Desert Red, were introduced during the mid-sixties and the company enjoyed a period of financial security.

The purchase of the Tiffin factory by Continental Can Company took place in 1966, followed by the sale to Interpace Corporation, parent company of Franciscan China in 1968. Several new Crystal lines were added to the Tiffin pattern listing during this time, and this ware was marketed under the Franciscan label. The final sale of the Tiffin Glass Company took place in May, 1979, to Towle Silversmiths. One year later production ceased; however, Towle sold inventory and operated a portion of the facility as a decorating shop until October, 1984, when all business came to a close at the Glasshouse located at Fourth Avenue and Vine Street.

A major contributor of fine quality glassware for nearly a century, the Tiffin Glass Company left a remarkable legacy for all of us to enjoy and to preserve. As you page through this volume, you may develop a new appreciation for the talented and industrious creators of Tiffin ware, as well as for their exquisite creations.

Identification Guide

One of the qualities that Tiffin Glass is noted for is color. The Color Guide illustrates the colors that Tiffin used from 1940 to 1980 for its blown ware, but colors will sometimes vary from the true color in the Color Guide. This variation can be attributed to the thickness of the glass, the length of refiring time, or batch variances. As little as two ounces of an element or mineral was used to color a 2000-pound batch of glass. Ingredients had to be measured with extreme accuracy, as just a few extra grains could influence the color. The Color Guide can also help to identify a piece of Tiffin Glass, especially when the glass shape is unknown. However, collectors must remember that other companies' colors will also resemble Tiffin's.

The Optics Guide can also be used to help identify Tiffin Glass. These optics were made from the years 1940-1980 and included: Swedish, Tiffin, half-spiral, spiral, pinwheel, Kosta, 5-rib, 10-rib, bubble, and diamond. Tiffin Optic was the one most widely used during the Modern Era and is the easiest optic to identify.

An attempt has been made to organize this book by line numbers, decorations, and styles. Because of the diversity of pieces made by Tiffin Glass, some items could not be placed in just one category. These items can be found in more than one section of the book.

Line numbers and production dates are taken from company catalogs, interoffice correspondence, and catalog pages from *Tiffin Glassmasters, Book III* by Fred Bickenheuser. Although all items pictured in this book are Tiffin Glass pieces, some line numbers could not be attributed by the authors and are listed as unknown line numbers. The dates of production were also obtained from the above sources.

Words or phrases used within double quotation marks are the authors' terms and are used to name some lines when documentation was lacking. These names were derived from company descriptions of the pieces or are terms commonly used by glass collectors. Descriptive terms Flower Bowl, Flower Arranger, Flower Basket, and Vase may appear to be used interchangeably, especially for Empress items; however, the terms used in the caption are the ones found in company catalogs.

All color names are capitalized. When the world "Crystal" is capitalized, it refers to a color name rather than a characteristic of the glass.

Dimensions of items are measured across at the widest point, whether it be the diameter of a round piece, or the length of an oval, rectangular, or irregular piece. In most cases, the height is abbreviated as "h." These dimensions can vary from item to item, as most of the examples pictured were hand-fashioned.

Prices are listed in U.S. dollars in bold type at the end of the caption. Each item is priced using a value range. These values were derived from actual purchase prices, by prices seen at antiques shows and shops, or by rarity and desirability. The prices are listed in the order in which the respective pieces appear in the photo. These values are intended as a guide, and neither the authors nor the publisher are responsible for any transactions based on this guide.

Color Guide:
The Colors
of Tiffin

Crystal. Tiffin was known for fine quality glass and Crystal was Tiffin's primary annual production color.

Opal. Opal was produced in the early 1940s and reintroduced in 1957 as Milk Glass.

Amber. Amber was produced for a brief period in the early 1940s.

Cobalt Blue. Cobalt Blue was produced in the early 1940s and reintroduced for a brief period in 1961.

Copen Blue. Copen Blue was a popular color produced through the 1940s and again in the mid 1960s.

Killarney. A deep green, Killarney was introduced in 1948 and was produced through the 1950s.

Wistaria. Production of Wistaria began in the late 1940s and continued for approximately ten years. The color varies from a shade of pale pink to a deep rose.

Twilight. A lavender color, Twilight was produced from c. 1951-1980. Under fluorescent lighting the color changes to a pale blue.

Pine. Sometimes confused with Killarney, Pine is a lighter shade of green and was produced c. 1952-1956.

Cerulean. Cerulean is a pale blue color that was produced briefly c. 1956.

Wild Rose. Wild Rose is a pink color similar to Wistaria. It lacks, however, the reddish tones of Wistaria, c. 1956.

Rose Blush. Rose Blush was produced in a limited number of items in 1956.

Smoke. The color of Smoke varies and appears in shades of purple, gray and brown. Production years were c. 1959 through the 1970s.

Ruby. Used during the 1920s and 1930s, Ruby was reintroduced c. 1959.

Emerald Green. Emerald Green was produced only in 1959, for the Empress line.

Sapphire Blue. Sapphire Blue was introduced in 1959 and used for the Empress line.

Plum. Tiffin's Amethyst was re-introduced as Plum in 1961.

Golden Banana. Golden Banana, a deep honey-gold color, was introduced in 1961.

Citron Green. Citron Green, a bright yellow green, was produced in the mid 1960s.

Greenbriar. This avocado color was introduced, c. 1967.

Desert Red. A deep amber color with reddish tones, Desert Red was produced c. 1965-1970.

Empire Green. Introduced in 1961, Empire Green was used in the production of pressed and blown ware.

Persimmon. Persimmon was produced in the early 1970s and varies in color from yellow to red-orange.

Black. Tiffin's Black color, produced in the 1970s. is opaque in comparison to the translucent black from the 1925-1935 era.

Optics Guide

Optics were formed by the use of tools or molds to create a series of lines, circles, or patterns within the body of the glass object, such as a vase or bowl.

Swedish/Tiffin Optic. The term "Swedish Optic" was used from 1940 until July 1946 when the term "Tiffin Optic" was adopted in order to identify Tiffin Glass as American-made.

Half-Spiral Optic. The Half-Spiral Optic was used on a limited number of items in the 1940s.

Spiral Optic. Spiral Optic was used c. 1940-1970, primarily in the production of the #6041 Cornucopias.

Pinwheel Optic. Pinwheel Optic was formed using a spinner mold. Limited production took place in the 1940s.

Kosta Optic. The only documented usage of Kosta Optic is the #526 rose bowl, produced in the 1940s.

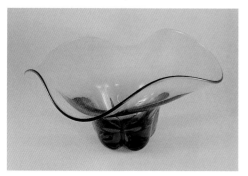

5 Rib Optic. 5 Rib Optic is comprised of five lobes molded in the base of the object, c. 1952.

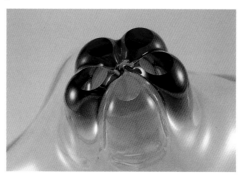

Detail of 5 Rib Optic

10 Rib Optic. Also known as deep rib optic, the 10 Rib Optic was formed using a spinner mold which created ten curved ridges. This optic, developed by Paul Williams, was widely used from 1940 through the 1970s.

Detail of 10 Rib Optic

Bubble Optic. Bubble Optic is a series of bubbles throughout the body of the glass object, c. 1952.

Diamond Optic. Diamond Optic was used in the 1920s and 1930s and also in the early 1960s.

11

The distinguishing feature of the 17350 line is the ball stem, used from the early to mid 1940s. Known colors in this line are Crystal, Cobalt Blue, Opal, Amber, and Copen Blue.

Right: Crystal #17350, 10" h. Teardrop Vase; 7-1/4" h. Sweet Pea Vase. Swedish Optic. **$40-65 each**

Below: Crystal #17350, 10" h. Teardrop Vase; #5972, 12-3/4" h. Flared Vase, Bubble ball stem; #5967, 11-1/2" h. Urn Vase, Bubble ball stem, all Half-Spiral Optic, c. 1940. **$100-125; $125-150; $125-150**

Crystal #17350, 9" Fruit Bowl, stained engraving; Swedish Optic #17350 4" h. Candleholder, engraved foot, faceted ball stem. **$65-85; $45-65**

Crystal #17350, 10" Handled Fruit Bowl, applied handles, Swedish Optic. **$200-225**

Opal #17350, 9-1/2" h.
Globe Vase, c. 1940.
$175-225

Amber #17350, 7-1/2" h. Sweet Pea
Vase, Crystal ball connector, Swedish
Optic. **$65-90**

Left: Amber #17350, 9" h. Flared
Vase, Crystal ball connector, Swedish
Optic. c. 1940. **$65-90**

Cobalt Blue #17350, 4" h.
Candleholder; 9" h. Flared Vase,
Crystal ball connectors, c. 1942. **$90-
110; $175-200**

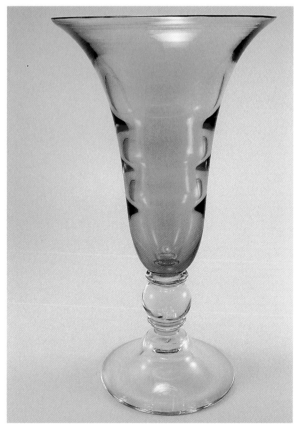

Wistaria, 11-3/4" h. Flared Vase, Crystal foot and ball connector, Tiffin Optic, unknown line number, c. 1950. **$225-275**

Top left: Copen Blue #17350, 10-1/4" h. Vase; 10-1/2" h. Bud Vase; 10-1/4" h. Daisy Vase; 9" h. Flared Vase. Crystal ball connectors, Swedish Optic. **$75-100; $45-65; $75-100; $65-85**

Copen Blue #17350, 9-1/4" h. Tub Vase; 6" Compote, Crystal ball connectors; #17383, 7-1/2" h. Sweet Pea Vase, Crystal Bubble ball connector. Swedish Optic, c. 1940. **$75-100; $50-75; $75-100**

Top right: Copen Blue #17350, 6" Compote, Crystal ball connector, fitted with sterling silver base, Swedish Optic. **$100-135**

14

Chapter 2
17430 Line

The 17430 line was produced c. 1945-1970. The distinctive feature is the hand-fashioned 4-part foot, which is configured from a gob of glass. Colors produced in this line were Crystal, Copen Blue, Killarney, Wistaria, Twilight, Pine, Cerulean, Wild Rose, Citron, Desert Red, and Greenbriar.

Above: Crystal #17430, 4" Cream and Sugar, applied feet and handles, Tiffin Optic. **$50-70 set**

Crystal #17430, 6" h. Rose Bowl; 8" Centerpiece Bowl, applied feet, Tiffin Optic. **$40-65 each**

Killarney #17430, 7" Bowl, flared rim, applied Crystal foot. **$115-135**

Killarney #17430, 6-3/8" Compote; 12" Centerpiece Bowl; 8" Centerpiece Bowl, applied Crystal feet. **$65-85; $110-130; $85-105**

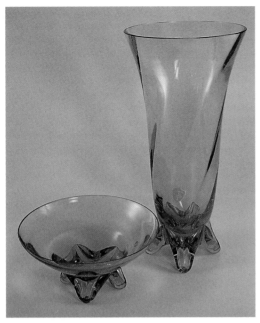

Far left: Wistaria #17430, 6-3/8" Compote, applied foot, Tiffin Optic; #17430 12-3/4" h. Flared Vase, applied foot, Half-Spiral Optic, c. 1950. **$85-115; $200-250**

Left: Wistaria #17430, applied feet, Tiffin Optic: 12-3/4" h. Flared Vase; 9" h. Flared Vase; 9-1/4" h. Teardrop Vase; 6" h. Sweet Pea Vase, c. 1950. **$200-225; $175-200; $175-200; $150-175**

Far left: Wistaria #17430, 12-3/4" h. Flared Vase; #17430, 8" Centerpiece Bowl, applied feet, Tiffin Optic, c. 1950. **$175-225; $150-200**

Left: Wistaria #17430, 10-1/4" h. Daisy Vase; 6" h. Sweet Pea Vase, applied feet Tiffin Optic, c. 1950. **$150-200; $175-225**

Wistaria #510, 7" h. Bowl; #17430, 9-1/4" Gardenia Bowl, applied foot. Tiffin Optic, c. 1950. **$150-200 each**

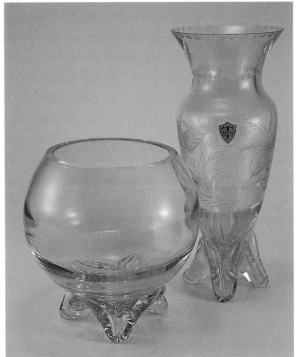

Above: Twilight #1
(catalogs also list this
piece as #17430),
10-1/2" h. Hurricane
Vase, applied foot;
#17430, 10-1/4" h.
Daisy Vase, applied
foot, "Leaf and Floral"
engraving, Tiffin Optic.
$175-225; $150-200

Above: Twilight
#17430, applied feet,
Tiffin Optic; 6-1/4"
Large Rose Bowl;
10-1/4" h. Daisy Vase,
engraved Parkwood by
Fred Windstine. **$185-
205; $250-275**

Right: Twilight #17430,
applied feet, Tiffin
Optic; 8" Centerpiece
Bowl, "Leaf" engraving
by Alyce Goetz. **$175-
200**

Twilight #17430, 9" h. Teardrop Vase, applied foot, Tiffin
Optic, engraved and acid polished. **$185-210**

Above: A detail of the engraving.

17

Pine #17430, applied Crystal feet: 9-1/4" h. Teardrop Vase; 6" h. Sweet Pea Vase, Bubble Optic, c. 1952. **$200-250 each**

Cobalt Blue #5859, 7" h. Flip Vase; Crystal #17430, 12-3/4" h. Flared Vase, applied Cobalt Blue foot, Tiffin Optic. **$85-110; $125-150**

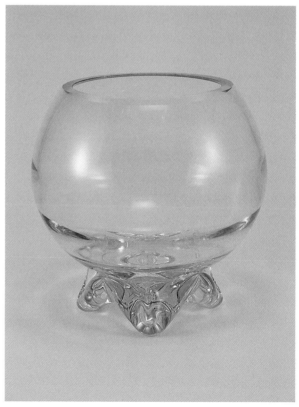

Wild Rose #17430, applied feet, Tiffin Optic; 12-3/4" h. Flared Vase; 6-3/8" Compote. Twelve items were offered in Wild Rose in a 1956 catalog. The vase sold for $4.25, and the compote for $3.00. **$125-150; $50-75**

Cerulean #17430, 6" h. Rose Bowl; 12-3/4" h. **$100-125**

Right: Copen Blue #17340 , applied feet, Tiffin
Optic: 6" h. Medium Rose Bowl; 9" h. Teardrop Vase,
"Leaf and Floral"engraving. **$65-85; $95-120**

Bottom left: Citron Green #6467, 5" Olive Dish,
applied handle; #17430, 7-1/2" h. Flared Vase, applied
foot; #17430, 6" h. Sweet Pea Vase, applied foot. Tiffin
Optic, c. 1965. **$50-70; $65-90; $65-90**

Bottom right: Citron Green #17430, 12" h. Centerpiece Bowl, applied foot, Tiffin Optic, c. 1965. **$65-90**

Desert Red, Citron Green #17430,
11-1/4" h. Flared Vases, applied feet,
Tiffin Optic, c. 1965. **$85-110 each**

Right: Crystal #6422, 11" h. Gladiola Vase with heavy applied foot, Tiffin Optic, c. 1948 (also known in Killarney). **$125-150**

Desert Red #17430, 8" Centerpiece Bowl, applied foot, Tiffin Optic, "Deer and Pine Tree" engraving by Clyde King. **$85-110**

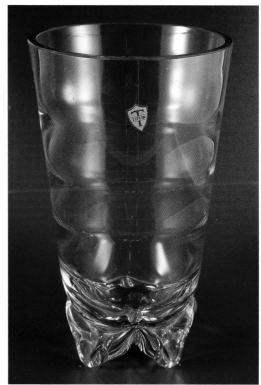

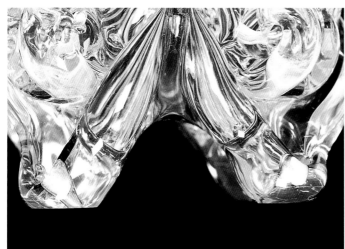

Center left: Greenbriar #17430, 8" Centerpiece Bowl, applied Crystal foot, Tiffin Optic, "Leaf" engraving, c. 1967. **$85-110**

Bottom left: Detail of heavy applied foot.

Center right: Detail of previous photo

Bottom right: Crystal #6433, 8" Fruit Bowl, c. 1965. Also known in Copen Blue. The foot is similar to the #17430 foot. **$125-150**

Chapter 3
Cellini Line

The Cellini line was produced from 1947 to the mid 1950s, with limited production in the 1960s. The distinctive characteristic is the delicate open work stem, which required the expertise of skilled craftsmen.

Left: Cellini advertisement taken from a 1947 *House Beautiful Magazine*.

Crystal 7" h. Candleholders, unknown line number; #6067 12" Bowl, Tiffin Optic, c. 1947. **$200-250 pair, $185-235**

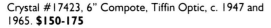

Crystal #17423, 6" Compote, Tiffin Optic, c. 1947 and 1965. **$150-175**

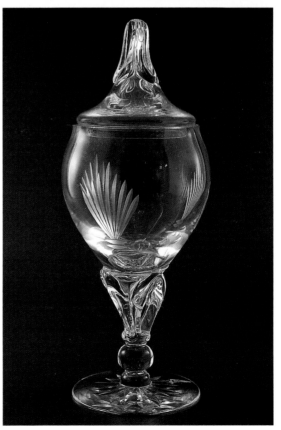

Crystal #17423, 14" h. Covered Candy Jar, applied finial, c. 1947. Blown by Oscar Theller. **$175-225**

22

Killarney with Crystal Trim
#17523, 11" h. Chalice
Vase, c. 1948. **$250-300**

Killarney with Crystal Trim
#17523, 10-3/4" h. Flared
Vase, c. 1948. **$250-300**

Killarney with Crystal Trim #17523, 13-1/4" h. Urn Vase,
c. 1948. **$250-300**

Wistaria with
Crystal Trim
#17423, 11-1/2"
h. Candy Jar,
applied finial, Tiffin
Optic, c. 1947-
1955. This candy
jar wholesaled for
$5.75 in 1955.
$275-325

Crystal, 14" h.
Vase, unknown
line number.
$200-250

Crystal #6220, 7-1/2" Bowl, "Leaf and Floral" engraving, c. 1947. **$250-300**

Citron Green #17423, 6-1/4" h. Candleholders; #17423 6"
Compote, Tiffin Optic, c. 1965. **$225-275 pair; $175-225**

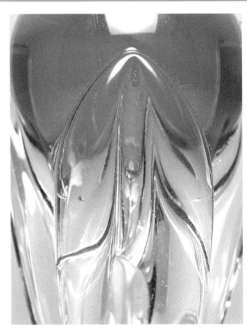

Crystal #17423, 6-1/4" h. Candleholders,
c. 1965. **$200-250 pair**

Copen Blue and Crystal #17423, 6-1/4" h.
Candleholders, c. 1965. **$250-300 pair**

Detail of Candleholder.

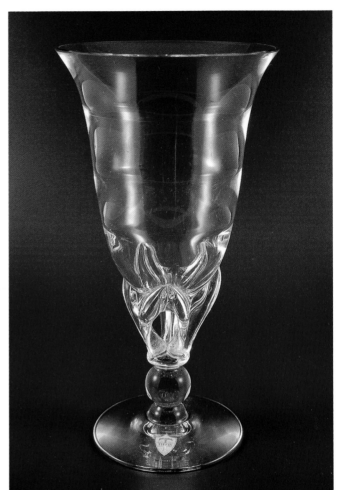

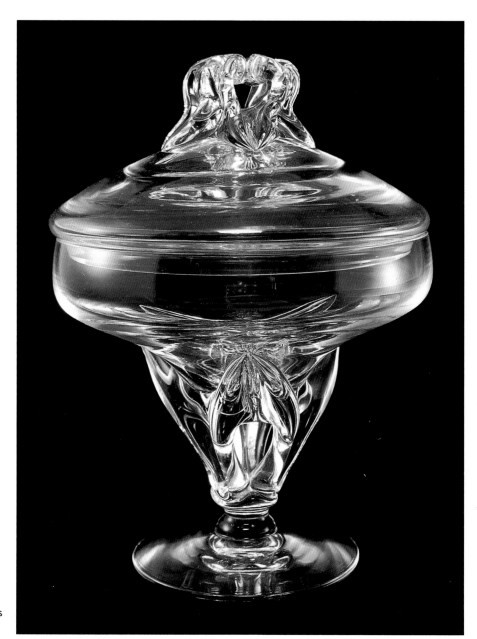

Crystal #17523, 8-1/2" h.
Covered Candy Box with
applied Crown finial, Tiffin
Optic, c. 1947-1955. 1955
catalog wholesale price was
$5.25. **$225-275**

Opposite:

Top Left:Crystal #6218, 13-1/2"
h. Covered Urn Vase, applied
Crown finial, Tiffin Optic, c.
1947. **$300-350**

Bottom left: Crystal #6418, 12"
h. Aster Vase, Tiffin Optic, c.
1952. **$250-300**

Top right: Crystal #17523,
13-1/4" h. Urn Vase, Tiffin Optic.
$225-275

Bottom right: Ruby and Crystal,
11" h. Chalice Vase, unknown line
number. **$400-450**

Wistaria and Crystal #17523, 8" h. Covered Candy Box with applied Crown finial, Tiffin Optic, c. 1947-1955. 1955 catalog wholesale price was $6.50. **$275-325**

Crystal #17523, 8" h. Covered Candy Box, applied finial, Tiffin Optic, c. 1947-1955. **$175-225**

Cobalt Blue and Crystal #17523, 13-1/2" h. Hurricane Vase. **$275-325**

Crystal #6217, 12-1/2" h. Vase, c. 1947. **$200-250**

Crystal #6228, 10-1/2" h. Bowl, c. 1947. **$200-250**

Far left: Wistaria and Crystal #17523, 10-3/4" h. Flared Vase, Tiffin Optic, c. 1947-1955. **$275-325**. Left: Wistaria #17523, 12" h. Bud Vase. **$175-225**

Above: Detail of Bud Vase.

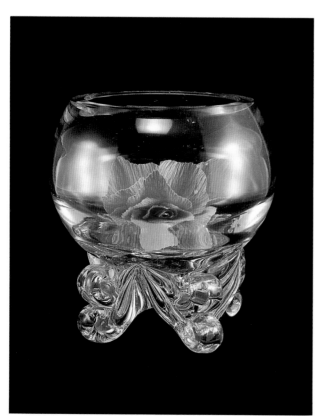

Crystal, 6" h. Rose Bowl, Tiffin Optic, unknown line number, c. 1947. **$125-175**

Crystal #6433, 8" Fruit Bowl, Tiffin Optic. **$175-225**

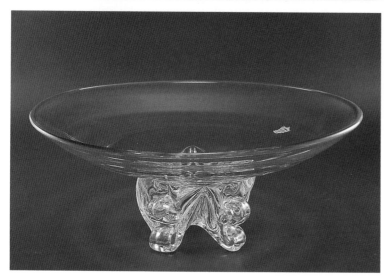

Crystal #6462, 13-1/4" Centerpiece Bowl, Tiffin Optic c. 1947-1965. This Cellini foot was also identified in the "Tiffin Modern" 1965 catalog as DaVinci. **$175-225**

Copen Blue #6433, 8" Fruit Bowl, Tiffin Optic, c. 1965. **$275-325**

Opposite: Crystal #6421, 7-3/4" Bowl, all-over "Leaf and Floral" type engraving. **$500-700**

United States Patent Office drawing of a vase, filed March 9, 1951 and issued November 27, 1951.

United States Patent Office drawing of a footed bowl, filed March 9, 1951 and issued November 27, 1951.

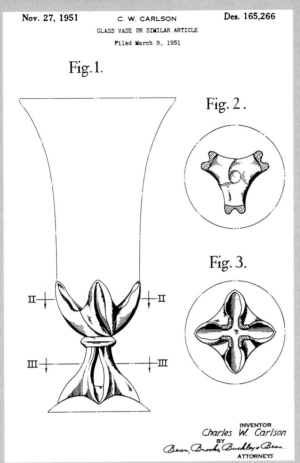

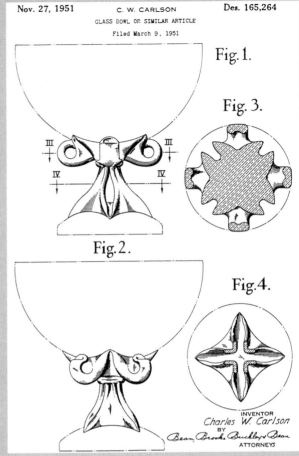

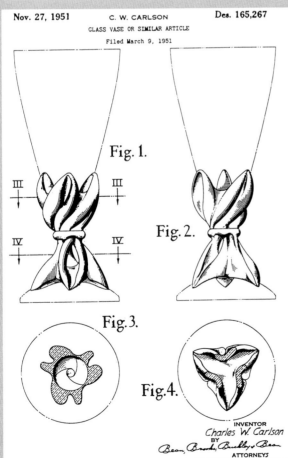

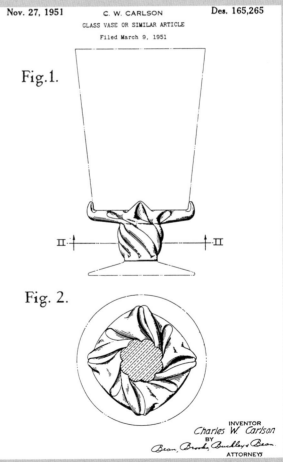

United States Patent Office drawing of a vase, filed March 9, 1951 and issued November 27, 1951.

United States Patent Office drawing of a vase, filed March 9, 1951 and issued November 27, 1951.

Chapter 4
Applied Trim

Applied decoration was used during the 1940 to 1950 era. These items are considered rare, as only a minimal number were produced.

Top left: Crystal #17375, 12" h. Urn Vase, applied handles; #17375, 10" h. Teardrop Vase, applied handles, "Leaf" engraving. **$125-175; $150-200**

Bottom left: Crystal #17385, 9" h. Flared Vase with applied Tear handles, Swedish Optic; #17375 9-1/2" h. Tub Vase, applied handles, Swedish Optic, c. early '40s. **$125-175 each**

Top right: Detail of engraving.

Bottom right: Crystal #17375, 9" h. Flared Vases with applied handles, Swedish Optic. **$125-175 each**

Crystal, #43, 10-1/2" h. Vase, #17350, 12" h. Daisy Vase with applied handles, c. 1940. **$60-85; $125-175**

Crystal, 5-3/4" h. Vase, applied handles, Swedish Optic, unknown line number. **$75-100**

Crystal, 6-3/4" h. Rose Bowl with 4 applied "leaves," Swedish Optic, unknown line number. **$125-175**

Crystal #5859, 10-3/4" h. Flip Vase with 3 applied "leaves." **$100-125**

Right: Wistaria #6255, 8-1/2" h. Vase with applied "leaves" on base, Tiffin Optic, c. 1951. (This vase was also made without the applied "leaves.") **$200-250**

Below: Crystal, 13-1/2" Centerpiece Bowl, blown base with applied "fingers," unknown line number, c. 1953. **$125-150**

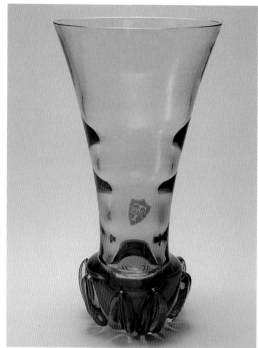

Above: Crystal, 10-1/2" h. Vase with applied green "leaves," unknown line number. This piece was purchased from the Archives Room when the factory was closing. The foot of the Vase is unfinished. **$125-150**

Above right: Crystal #17508, 9-1/2" h. Flared Vase with green "Loop" appliqué, Tiffin Optic; Crystal, 9-1/4" h. Vase with green "Loop" appliqué, unknown line number. **$175-225 each**

Right: Crystal, 8" Shallow Bowl with 2 applied green streamers, engraved bowl, unknown line number, c. 1952. **$115-140**

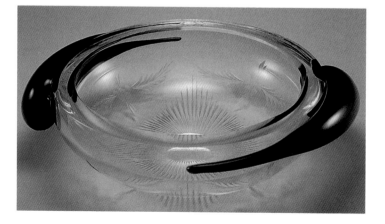

Chapter 5
"Scallop Edge"

To form the "Scallop Edge," the rim was sheared and turned down to create a decorative overlapping trim. This treatment was developed in 1952, and all "Scallop Edge" pieces are considered very rare.

Killarney, 10-1/2" h. "Scallop Edge" Vase, unknown line number, c. 1952. **$225-275**

Twilight #58, 8" "Scallop Edge" Bowl, in Jan. 8, 1953 Glass Trade Show. **$250-300**

Twilight #51, 5" h. "Scallop Edge" Rose Bowl, Bubble Optic, in Jan. 8, 1953 Glass Trade Show. **$300-350**

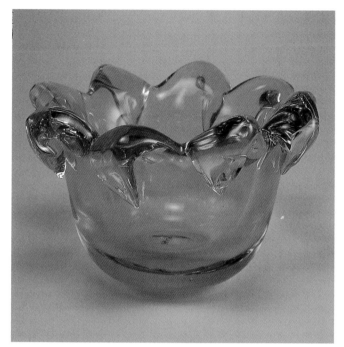

Twilight #55, 12" "Scallop Edge" Center Bowl, 10 Rib Optic base, in Jan. 8, 1953 Glass Trade Show. **$250-300**

Chapter 6
Blown Foot

The blown foot is less common than the typical disc-shaped foot. Production years were c. 1940-1955.

Twilight, 9-1/2" Oval Bowl, with applied blown foot, unknown line number. **$125-150**

Twilight, 7" d. Compotes, with blown feet, unknown line number, c. 1954. **$125-150 each**

Twilight, 10-3/4" Center Bowl, blown foot, unknown line number. **$150-175**

Top left: Crystal #5933, 7" Blown Compote, with blown foot, Swedish Optic, c. 1940. **$75-100**

Bottom left: Crystal #5934, 10-3/4" h. Hurricane Lamp Vases, with blown Copen Blue feet, Swedish Optic, c. 1940. **$150-175 each**

Top right: Crystal #5934, 10-1/2" h. Hurricane Lamp Vase, with blown foot, c. 1940. **$75-100**

Chapter 7
"3 Leaf Stem"

The "3 Leaf Stem" consists of a molded three part connector formed around the base of the object, c. 1950.

Right: Crystal, 12-1/4" h. Vase, "3 Leaf Stem" connector, Tiffin Optic, unknown line number, c. 1950. **$85-115**

Far right: Crystal, 9-1/2" h. Teardrop Vase, "3 Leaf Stem" connector, Tiffin Optic, unknown line number, c. 1950. **$85-115**

Left: Killarney, 13-1/4" h. 7-1/2 oz. Cordial Decanter, with Crystal base and stopper, unknown line number, c. 1950. **$150-175**

Far left: Crystal, 13-1/4" h. 7-1/2 oz. Cordial Decanter, with stopper, "3 Leaf Stem;" 7" h. Sweet Pea Vase, "3 Leaf Stem." Unknown line numbers, c. 1950. **$85-115 each**

Chapter 8
5 Rib Optic

Top right: Twilight #6426, 6" d. Ash Tray, 5 Rib Optic, c. 1952. **$125-150**

Center right: Wistaria, 6-1/2" Ash Tray, 10 Rib Optic, unknown line number; #6426, 6-3/4" d. Ash Tray, 5 Rib Optic. **$150-175 each**

Bottom right: Wistaria, 6-1/2" Rose Bowl, 5 Rib Optic, unknown line number. **$250-300**

Top left: Twilight #6263, 8" h. Crimped Vase, 5 Rib Optic, c. 1952. **$185-235**

Bottom left: Wistaria #6264, 9" h. Vase, 5 Rib Optic, c. 1952. **$225-275**

Cobalt Blue #5966, 8" h. Heavy Blown
Vase, 10 Rib Optic, c. 1942. **$225-275**

Below: Iridescent #5966, 8" h. Heavy Blown Vase, 10 Rib Optic, c. 1950. This was an experimental item. **$150-175**

Opposite:
Top left: Wistaria #5966, 8" h. Heavy Blown Vase, 10 Rib Optic, c. 1950. **$275-325**
Top right: Twilight #5475, 4" h. Rose Bowl, 10 Rib Optic, c. 1955; #5966, 10" h. Heavy Blown Vase, 10 Rib Optic, c. 1951. **$200-250 each**
Bottom left: Crystal #5984, 12-1/2" h. Heavy Blown Vase, 10 Rib Optic; #5966, 8" h. Heavy Blown Vase, 10 Rib Optic. **$125-150 each**
Bottom right: Crystal with Cobalt Blue, 9-1/2" h. Vase, 10 Rib Optic, unknown line number. **$175-225**

Twilight #5477, 15-1/2" Free Form Bowl,
10 Rib Optic. **$175-225**

Twilight, 7" h. Vase, 10 Rib Optic, unknown line number,
c. 1954. **$200-250**

Twilight #5461, 8" Oval Bowl, 10 Rib Optic, c. 1955.
$150-175

Center left: Twilight, 7-1/2" h. Basket, applied handle, 10
Rib Optic; 7-1/2" h. offhand Basket, 2 twisted handles.
These baskets were not production items. **$175-225
each**

Twilight #5471, 6-1/4" h. Rose Bowl, 10 Rib Optic; #5461, 9" Oval Bowl,
10 Rib Optic, c. 1955. **$150-200; $150-175**

Wistaria, 4" Shallow Bowl, 10 Rib Optic, unknown line number, c. 1955; #5475, 4" Small Rose Bowl, 10 Rib Optic, c. 1955. **$175-225; $250-300**

Wistaria #5467, 11" Teardrop Bowl, 10 Rib Optic, unknown line number, c. 1950. **$200-250**

Wistaria #5453, 8-1/2" Heart Shape Ash Tray, 10 Rib Optic. **$200-250**

Wistaria #6260, 13" Gardenia Bowl, 10 Rib Optic. **$200-250**

Wistaria #5986, 13" Bowl, Pinwheel Optic, c. 1950. Pinwheel Optic is made from a 10 Rib Optic mold. **$200-250**

Killarney, 11-1/2" Flower Bowl, with Crystal 10 Rib Optic base, unknown line number. **$175-225**

Smoke #5466, 11" Square Ash Tray, with 4 cigar rests, 10 Rib Optic, c. 1960s. **$50-75**

Plum #33, 5-1/4" h. Square Vase, 10 Rib Optic; the 1961 Catalog wholesale price was $7.50. **$125-150**

Plum #5477, 15-1/2" Free Form Bowl, 10 Rib Optic, c. 1961. **$125-150**

Desert Red #1, 8" Ash Tray, 4 cigar rests, 10 Rib Optic, c. 1965. **$100-125**

Copen Blue, 13-1/4" h. Vase, 2 handles, 10 Rib Optic, unknown line number, c. 1940s. **$150-200**

47

Greenbriar #1, 8" Ash Tray, 4 cigar rests, 10 Rib Optic; #17430, 9-1/4" h. Teardrop Vase, applied Crystal foot, Tiffin Optic, c. 1967. **$50-75; $45-70**

Persimmon, 7" Bowl, 10 Rib Optic, unknown line number, c. 1970. **$30-55**

Persimmon #5461, 7" Oval Bowl, 10 Rib Optic. **$75-100**

Top: Persimmon #5461, 9" Oval Bowl, 10 Rib Optic, c. 1970. **$65-90**

Center: Empire Green #5477, 15" Free Form Bowl, 10 Rib Optic, c. 1970. **$45-70**

Right: Black #5461, 8" Oval Bowl, 10 Rib Optic, c. 1970. **$40-65**

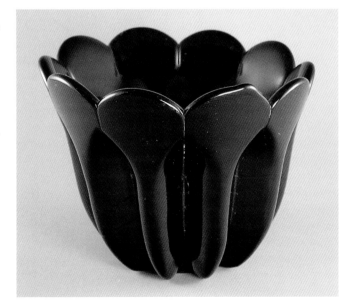

Chapter 10
Empress Line

The Empress line, introduced in 1959, is hand-fashioned Modern cased glass and was produced in seventy-five different styles. The original color combinations were: Ruby and Crystal, Emerald Green and Crystal, Smoke and Crystal, Sapphire Blue and Crystal, and Twilight and Smoke. Twilight and Green replaced the Emerald Green and Crystal combination in 1960. Empress was an extremely popular line and remains a favorite of collectors today.

Ruby and Crystal
Emerald Green and Crystal
Smoke and Crystal
Sapphire Blue and Crystal
Twilight and Smoke
Twilight and Green

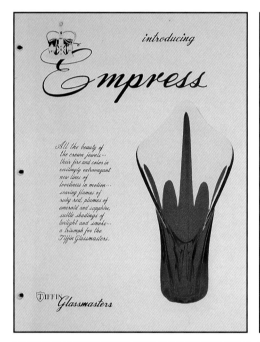

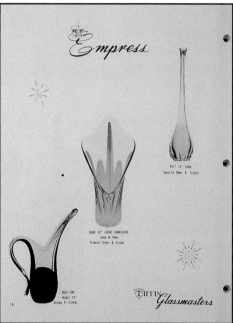

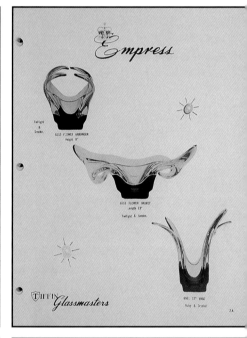

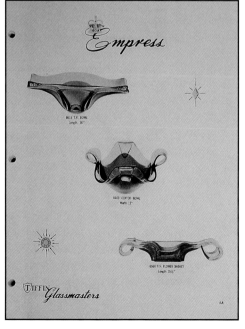

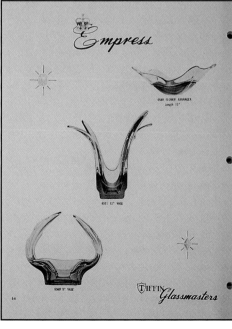

1959 Empress Catalog.

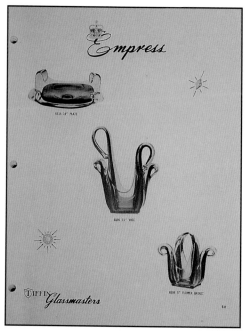

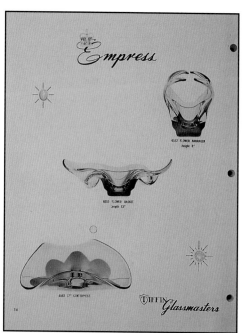

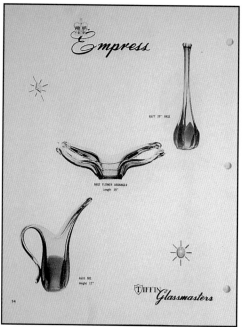

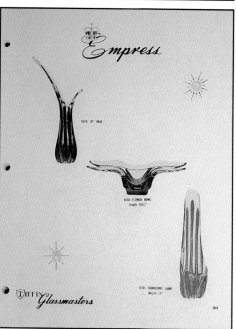

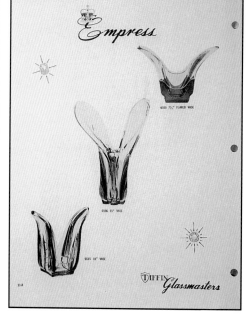

1959 Empress Catalog.

51

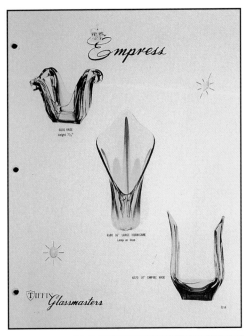

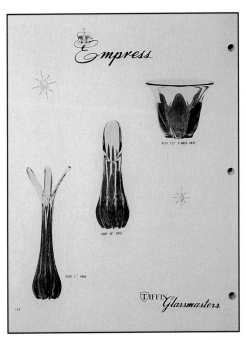

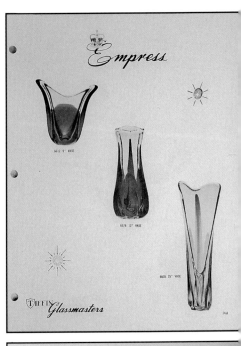

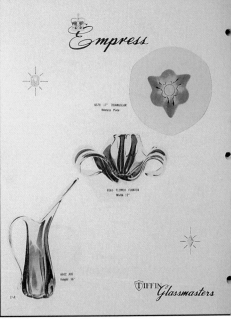

1959 Empress Catalog.

52

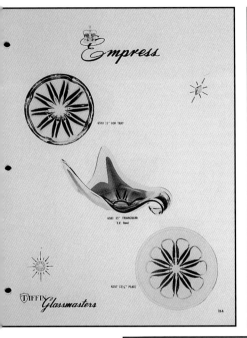

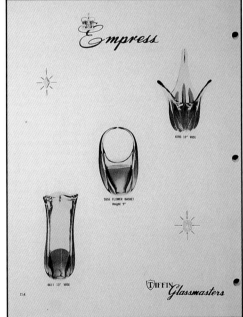

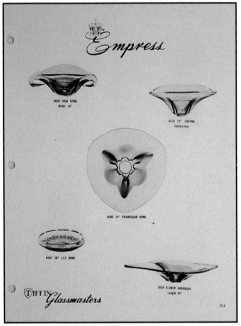

1959 Empress Catalog.

**Ruby
and
Crystal**

Ruby and Crystal
#6575, 7-1/2" Flared
Vase. **$200-250**

Ruby and Crystal #6553, 13" Flower Basket. **$200-250**

Opposite: Ruby and Crystal #6580, 16" h. Large Hurricane Vase.
$275-325

Ruby and Crystal
#6608, 23" Flower
Arranger. **$200-250**

Ruby and Crystal #6612, 8-1/4" h. Vase. **$150-200**

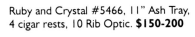

Ruby and Crystal #6557, 13-1/2" Plate, 10 Rib Optic. **$150-200**

Ruby and Crystal #6560, 16" h. Vase,
10 Rib Optic. **$200-250**

Ruby and Crystal , 26" Flower Arranger, unknown line number. **$200-250**

Ruby and Crystal #5477, 16-1/2" Free Form Bowl, 10 Rib Optic. **$200-250**

Ruby and Crystal #6607, 19" Flower Arranger. **$225-275**

Top: Ruby and Crystal #6616, 7-1/2" h. Vase. **$225-275**

Ruby and Crystal #6583, 17"
Centerpiece Bowl. **$200-250**

Ruby and Crystal #6602, 16" h. Jug,
interior satin finish. **$275-325**

Ruby and Crystal #6568, 26" Flower Arranger. **$200-250**

Ruby and Crystal #6594, 20" Flower Arranger. **$200-250**

Ruby and Crystal
#6552, 8" h.
Flower Arranger.
$225-275

Ruby and Crystal
#6577, 19" h.
Vase. **$150-200**

Ruby and Crystal #6599, 10" Ash Tray. **$275-325**

Opposite: Ruby and Crystal #6574, 9" h. Vase. **$200-250**

Ruby and Crystal #6551,
12" h. Vase. **$200-250**

Ruby and Crystal #6563, 12" Flower Floater, 10 Rib Optic. **$225-275**

Ruby and Crystal #5556, 8" h.
Flower Basket. **$200-250**

Ruby and Crystal #6559,
18" h. Vase, 10 Rib Optic.
$200-250

Emerald Green and Crystal

Top left: Emerald Green and Crystal #6602, 15" h. Jug. **$175-225**

Top right: Emerald Green and Crystal #6553, 13" Flower Basket. **$150-200**

Emerald Green and Crystal #6552, 8" h. Flower Arranger. **$150-200**

Above: Emerald Green and Crystal
#6603, 12" Center Bowl. **$150-200**

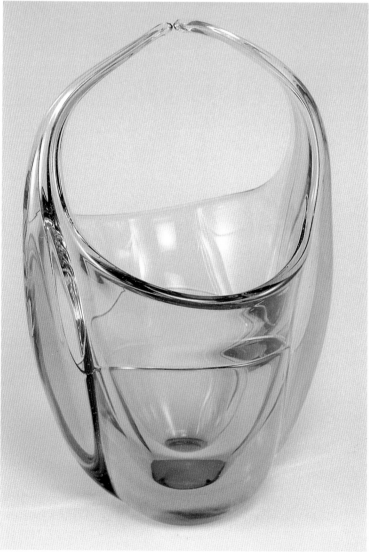

Emerald Green and Crystal #5556,
9" h. Flower Basket. **$150-200**

Emerald Green and Crystal #6567, 9-1/2" h. Vase. **$150-200**

Emerald Green and Crystal #6586, 9" Ash Tray. **$125-175**

Emerald Green and Crystal #6608, 20-3/4" Flower Arranger. **$150-200**

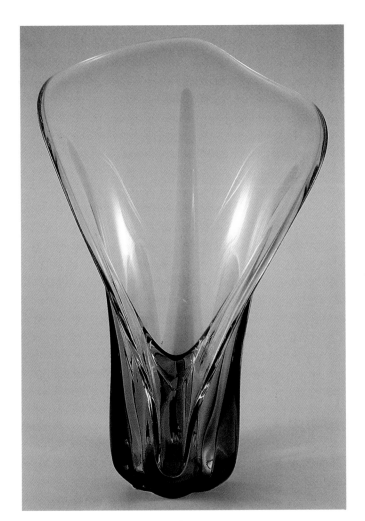

Smoke and Crystal

Smoke and Crystal #6551, 12" h. Vase. **$125-175**

Top: Smoke and Crystal #6580, 16"
h. Large Hurricane Vase. **$125-175**

Bottom: Smoke and Crystal #6599,
10" Ash Tray. **$125-175**

Below: Sapphire Blue and Crystal #6563, 12" Flower Floater, 10 Rib Optic. **$150-200**

Center left: Sapphire Blue and Crystal #6591, 8" Gardenia Bowl. **$125-175**

Sapphire Blue and Crystal

Sapphire Blue and Crystal #6617, 22" Aladdin's Lamp. **$150-200**

Top right: Sapphire Blue and Crystal #6602, 16" h. Jug. **$175-225**

Sapphire Blue and Crystal #6595, 11" h. Vase. **$175-225**

Sapphire Blue and Crystal #6598, 9" h. Flower Basket. **$150-200**

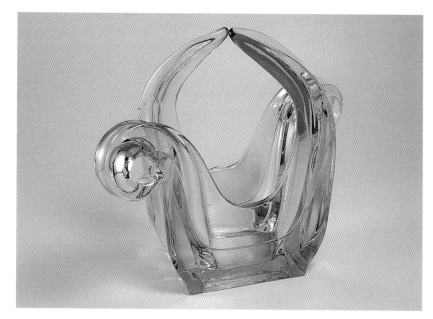

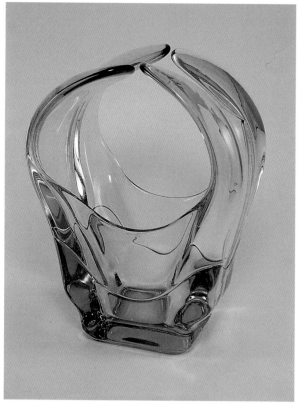

Sapphire Blue and Crystal #5466, 11" Square Ash Tray,
4 cigar rests, 10 Rib Optic. **$125-175**

Sapphire Blue and Crystal #6552, 8" h.
Flower Arranger. **$150-200**

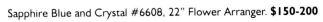

Sapphire Blue and Crystal #6586, 9" Ash Tray. **$125-175**

Sapphire Blue and Crystal #6608, 22" Flower Arranger. **$150-200**

Sapphire Blue and Crystal #6609, 10" Ram Bowl. **$125-175**

Sapphire Blue and Crystal #6569, 9" h. Vase. **$150-200**

Twilight and Smoke #6570, 14" h.
Empire Vase. **$200-250**

Twilight
and
Smoke

Twilight and Smoke #6557, 13-1/2"
Plate. **$175-225**

Twilight and Smoke #6551, 12" h. Vases. **$200-250 each**

Opposite:

Top: Twilight and Smoke #6599, 10" Ash Tray. **$175-225**

Bottom left: Twilight and Smoke #6559, 15-1/2" h. Vase, 10 Rib Optic. **$200-250**

Bottom right: Twilight and Smoke #6578, 12" h. Vase. **$175-225**

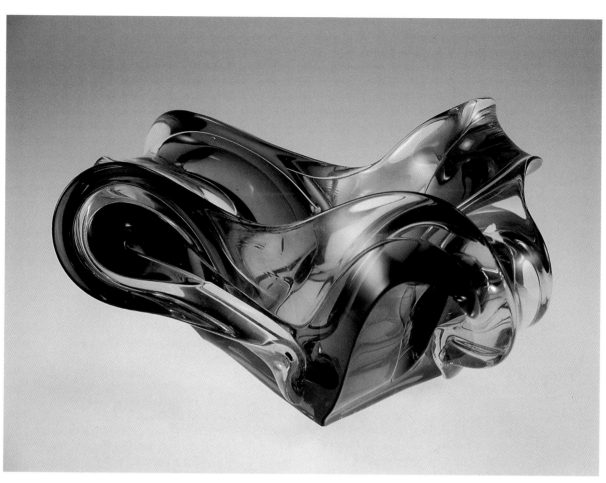

Twilight and Smoke #6553, 15" Flower Baskets. **$200-250 each**

Top: Twilight and Smoke #6561, 9" Bowl, 10 Rib Optic. **$175-225**

Twilight and Smoke #6598, 9" h. Flower Basket. **$200-250**   Twilight and Smoke #6565, 19" h. Vase, 10 Rib Optic. **$175-225**

Twilight and Smoke #5466, 11" Ash Tray, 4 cigar rests, 10 Rib Optic. **$175-225**

Twilight and Smoke, #6556, 7" Candleholders. **$150-200 pair**

Twilight and Smoke #6555, 7-1/2" h. Flared Vase. **$200-250**

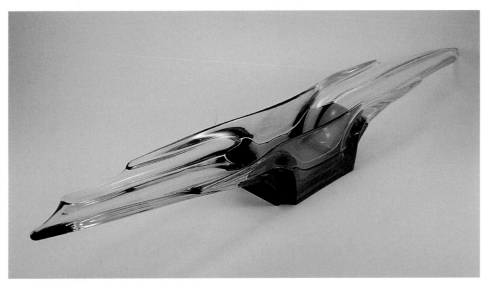

Twilight and Smoke #6568, 25" Flower Arranger. **$200-250**

Twilight and Smoke
#6564, 5-1/2" h.
Rose Bowl, 10 Rib
Optic. **$175-225**

Twilight and Smoke #6550, 15-1/2" Flower Bowl. **$200-250**

79

Twilight and Green

Twilight and Green #6551, 12" h. Vase. **$250-300**

Top left: Twilight and Green #6558, 19" h. Vase, 10 Rib Optic. **$250-300**

Top right: Detail of Twilight and Green Vase.

Bottom left: Twilight and Green #6560, 12" h. Vase, 10 Rib Optic. **$250-300**

Bottom right: Twilight and Green #6554, 7-1/2" Ash Tray. **$200-250**

Produced in Empress molds, these look-alikes differ from the Empress Line as they are not cased glass but one solid color.

Above: Twilight #5550, 10" Ram Bowl, c. 1955. **$150-175**

Wistaria #5466, 11" Square Ash Tray, 4 cigar rests, 10 Rib Optic, c. 1950. **$175-225**

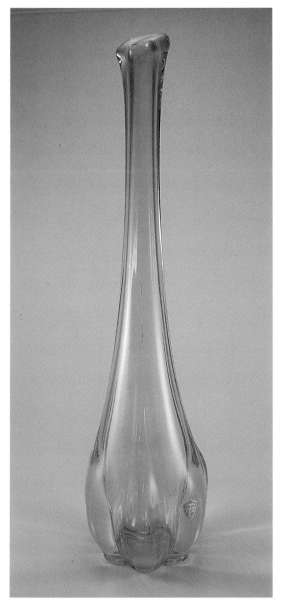

Twilight #6577, 20" h. Vase, made intermittently 1950s-1970s. **$125-150**

Smoke #6560, 16" h. Vase, 10 Rib Optic, c. 1960s. **$40-65**

Twilight #6576, 7" Rose Bowl. **$150-175**

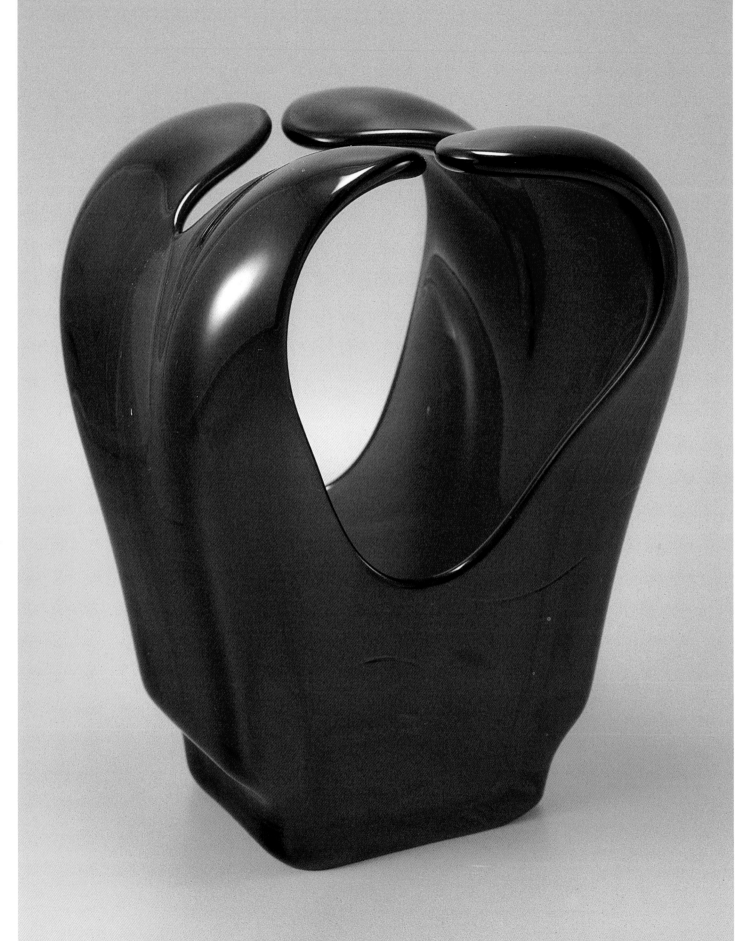

Golden Banana #6553, 14-1/2" Flower Arranger, c. 1962. **$125-150**

Opposite: Cobalt Blue #6552, 7-1/4"
h. Flower Arranger, c. 1961. **$125-175**

Plum #6553, 14-1/2" Flower Arranger, c. 1961. 1961 catalog
wholesale price was $7.00. **$125-150**

Cobalt Blue #6553, 14" Flower Arranger, c. 1961. **$225-275**

Next page:
Persimmon #6552, 7-3/4" h. Flower Arranger Vase. **$65-90**

Left: Persimmon #6551, 12" h. Vase. **$65-90**

Below: Persimmon #6550, 15-1/2" Flower Bowl. **$45-70**

Previous page:
Persimmon #6551, 12" h. Vase. **$65-90**

90

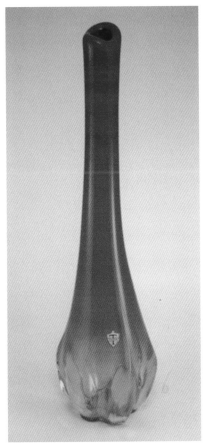

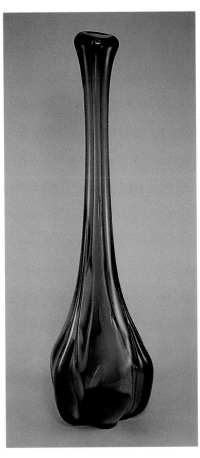

Persimmon #6577, 20"
h. Vase, with Opales-
cence, c. 1970. **$75-100**

Empire Green #6577,
24" h. Vase, c. 1970.
$40-65

Empire Green #6609, 10" Ram Bowl, c 1970. **$45-70**

The "Air Trap" technique was used for a very limited time, c. 1967. This treatment captures columns of air within the body of the object.

Crystal, 8" h. "Air Trap" Jug with applied handle, unknown line number, c. 1965. **$150-200**

Crystal, 9-3/4" h. "Air Trap" Vase, rolled and crimped rim, unknown line number, c. 1965. **$150-200**

Citron #15, 9" h. "Air Trap" Flip Vase, c. 1965. Also made in Copen Blue. **$175-225**

Top: Desert Red, 9" "Air Trap" Rolled Edge Bowl, unknown line number, c. 1965. **$175-225**

Chapter 13
Royale Line

Introduced in 1968, the Royale Line was comprised of twenty items. Some of the shapes were borrowed both from the Empress Line and from other shapes that were produced in the mid 1950s. Royale was produced in Crystal only, and each piece was sold in a red velvet-like "Royale" bag which was closed with a gold drawstring. Wholesale prices averaged $20.00 each in 1968.

1968 Royale Line Catalog.

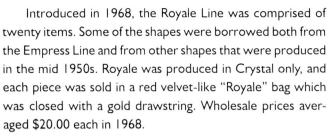

6822 5¼" VASE
An eye-appealing design fashioned in crystal for your prettiest floral bouquets.

6807 7⅛" FLARED VASE
A sculptured crystal jewel for your loveliest and most imaginative arrangements.

6801 10½" BOWL
A round crystal bowl ... is the simplicity of this centerpiece for fruits and flowers.

6802 7" FLOWER BOWL/Flower Floater
An excellent gift item ... perfect for candies and nuts.

6803 13" PLATE
A most useful item for your entertaining ... for sandwiches and hors d'oeuvres.

6804 11" LILY BOWL
Unlimited in its use ... an enchanting flower floater.

93

6810 13" TORTE PLATE (top)
Puritan in design . . .
for the most
discriminating hostess.

6811 10" SALAD BOWL
To compliment your
dining table . . .
for salads and fruits.

6805 ROSE BOWL
Tiffin has captured
refined elegance in this
decorative and
versatile flower bowl.

6806 ASH TRAY
An impressive and
useful gift . . . ideal for
an executive's desk
or for the most
fashionable home.

A new innovation in decorative and gift
items by Tiffin. A diversified selection of ash trays,
vases, torte plates, centerpieces, bowls,
bon bons and rose bowls to attract your customers.
Tiffin's moderately-priced ROYALE Line is destined
to become a pace setter. At a surprisingly-low
investment, your customers can enjoy the
excitement of crystal decorative accents in their
homes as designed by world-famous Tiffin.

6812 12" CENTERPIECE
Flawless in its purity
of line . . . refreshing
in its simplicity.

6809 8" FLARED VASE
A modern design and
cutting combined
to create a lovely vase
for your favorite
flowers.

6808 8" FLARED VASE
superbly fashioned
to blend the elements
of beauty and usefulness.

6814 FLOWER ARRANGER
An example of design excellence . . .
inspired by the natural beauty
of Tiffin Crystal.

1968 Royale Line Catalog.

94

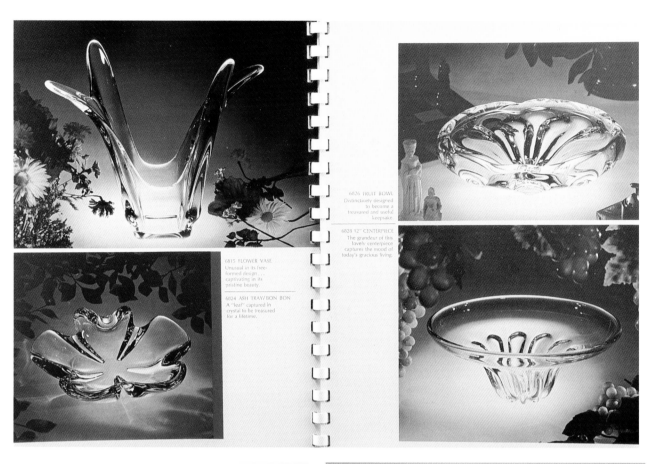

6826 FRUIT BOWL
Distinctively designed
to become a
treasured and useful
keepsake.

6828 12" CENTERPIECE
The grandeur of this
lovely centerpiece
captures the mood of
today's gracious living.

6815 FLOWER VASE
Unusual in its free-
formed design . . .
captivating in its
pristine beauty.

6824 ASH TRAY/BON BON
A "leaf" captured in
crystal to be treasured
for a lifetime.

6810 20" LILY VASE
Graceful in its elegance
and unique styling.

6816 ROSE BOWL
A jewel-like glow
accents the splendor
of this lovely
decorative piece.

10

Top & above: 1968 Royale Line
Catalog.

Crystal #6824, 9" Ash Tray/Bon Bon, Royale cloth bag in
background. **$50-75**

Crystal #6808, 8" h. Flared Vase. **$50-75**

Top right:
Crystal #6801, 10-1/2"
Bowl; #6809, 8" h.
Flared Vase; #6805, 6"
h. Rose Bowl. **$40-65;
$50-75; $50-75**

Crystal #6804, 11" Lily
Bowl. **$40-65**

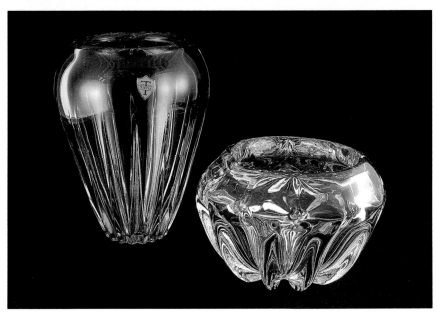

Crystal #6807, 7-1/2"
h. Flared Vase; #6816,
4-1/2" Rose Bowl.
$50-75 each

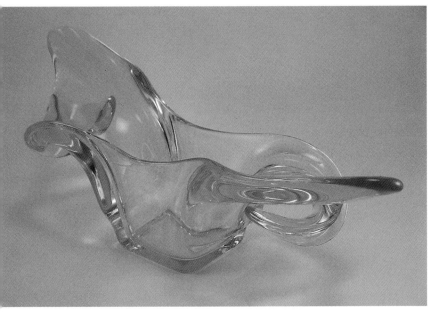

Chapter 14
Royale
Look-Alikes

Since the Royale line was derived from other lines and shapes, Royale look-alikes abound. The #6553 Flower Basket, #6551 Vase, #6560 Vase and the #6590 Ash Tray are shapes used in both the Empress and Royale lines. These same shapes can also be found in solid colors, which are neither the Crystal Royale line nor the cased glass Empress line. Most of the other Royale line shapes were also produced in the mid 1950s. These shapes are often found in Twilight or Crystal. The line numbers for the Royale look-alikes differ from the numbers designated for the 1968 Royale line.

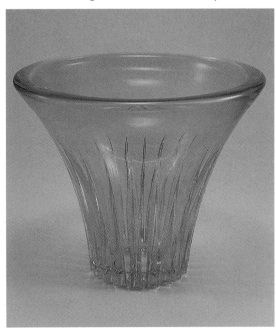

Above: Twilight #5567, 7" h. Flared Vase, c. 1955. **$150-175**

Top left: Twilight #5563, 7" Ash Tray, c. 1955. **$125-150**

Center left: Twilight #5562, 10" Fruit Bowl, c. 1955. **$150-175**

Bottom left: Twilight #6553, 16-1/4" Flower Basket. **$150-200**

97

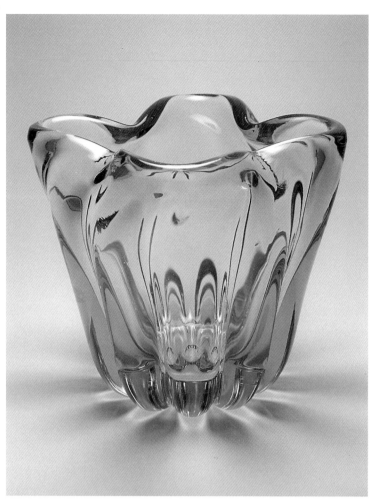

Opposite: Vase, 7-1/2" h., signed "Linda S. Cleve" and acid-stamped with Tiffin Shield mark. **$250-300**

Copen Blue #33, 6" h. Square Vase, c. 1965. **$125-175**

Persimmon #6590, 11" Ash Tray, 4 cigar rests, 10 Rib Optic. **$40-65**

Chapter 15
Linda Cleve

Linda Cleve was a young artist employed by Tiffin in the early 1970s. Her modernistic cased glass designs were non-production items that are sought by collectors today. Following a brief period of time spent at the Tiffin factory, Linda Cleve moved to the Fostoria Glass Company and continued designing glass there.

Vase, 7" h., signed Linda S. Cleve and acid stamped with Tiffin Shield mark; Vase, 9" h., signed "Linda Cleve". **$250-300 each.**

Opposite: Vase, 7-1/2" h., acid stamped with Tiffin Shield mark. **$250-300.**

Inkwell Paperweight, 4" h.. **$200-250**

Top right: Linda Cleve vase with a place setting of Franciscan China. The Tiffin factory was purchased by Interpace Corporation, parent company of Franciscan China. The photograph was taken at an early 1970s china and glass trade show.

Right: Linda Cleve goblet with a place setting of Franciscan China, from a company slide.

Chapter 16
Glass Trade Shows

The Tiffin Glass Company participated with other major glass manufacturers in displaying their new designs at various glass trade shows. As competition was keen, companies were constantly creating new designs to appeal to the attending sales representatives and, ultimately, to the buying public. Shows were held each year, beginning in the early 1900s.

Tiffin's participation in national china and glass shows was interrupted by the war, as stated in an announcement in the January 1944 issue of *Crockery and Glass Journal*. Tiffin resumed their involvement once the war ended.

Factory interoffice correspondence provided information covering the 1952, 1953 and 1954 glass trade shows held at Pittsburgh, Pennsylvania, and New York City. In order to maintain a position of leadership in the glass industry, new designs were introduced regularly, every six months, for these shows. This was an incredible accomplishment for both the company and the skilled glassworkers.

1954 Glass Trade Show. *Photo, Center for Archival Collections, Bowling Green State University. Copyright Bowling Green.*

January 3, 1952
Glass Trade Show

Included in the ninety new items that were made specifically for the glass trade show at Pittsburgh were: thirty-six vases, twenty bowls, and ten candlesticks. Seven Crown stem pieces were shown, along with four Manzoni foot items and a 5 Rib Optic bowl and vase. Two compotes and a candlestick featured Air Twist stems, and two candlesticks had a 4-part Leaf stem. A number of Bubble ball stem objects were made. Unusual and interesting treatments using color were seen on several new items. A Crystal #10 Swirl Optic Bowl, with a 10 Rib Optic base, had a blue scalloped rim. A Ring Stem with blue streamers was used on a 9" #16 Bowl made from a gardenia bowl mold. Blue was also used on the base of the four cast curled toes of a 8-1/2" #25 Vase.

Above: Twilight #5, 9-1/2" h. Vases, Crown Stem, Tiffin Optic. **$250-300 each**

Top right: Twilight #1, 8" Ash Tray, 4 crimps for cigar rests, cut in at base of bowl to form a ribbed foot, 10 Rib Optic. **$175-225**

Center right: Twilight #11, 10" Rectangular Bowl with Manzoni foot. **$175-225**

Bottom right: Wistaria #15, 10" Crimped Bowl, 5 Rib Optic. **$225-275**

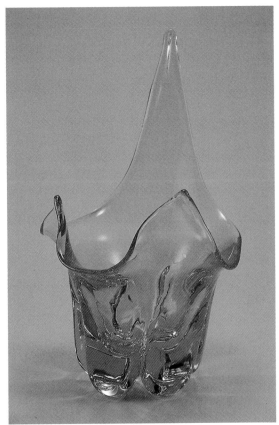

Twilight #32, 12-1/4" h. Vase, 5 Rib Optic. **$200-250**

Top left: Twilight #15, 12" Free Form Crimped Bowl, 5 Rib Optic. **$185-235**

Center left: Twilight #15, 7-1/4" h. Vase with Manzoni foot; #15, 9" h. Vase with Manzoni foot, Tiffin Optic (a 10-1/4" size in this shape was also produced). **$200-250; $225-275**

Bottom left: Twilight #33, 5-1/4" h. Square Vases, 10 Rib Optic. **$150-175 each**

Crystal #5, 9" Fruit Bowl, Crown stem, Tiffin Optic. **$200-250**

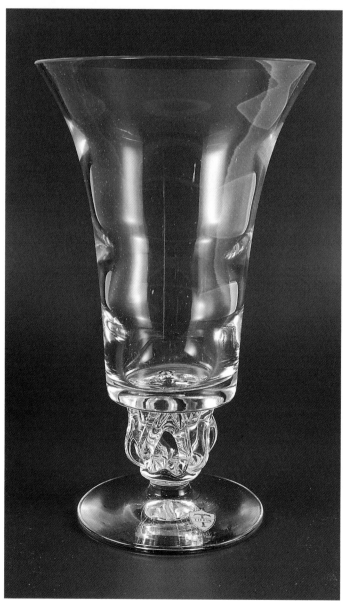

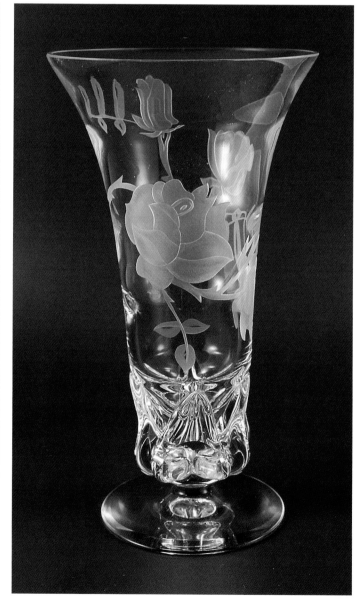

Crystal #24, 10-1/4" h. Flared Vase, Crown stem, Tiffin Optic.
$200-250

Crystal #13, 11-1/4" h. Flared Vase, Crown stem, Tiffin Optic, sand
carved Roses. **$250-300**

July 13, 1952 Glass Trade Show

Six months after the January show, seventy-two new items were shown at a glass trade show held in New York City on July 13, 1952. Vases and bowls once again comprised the majority of the new items designed to attract the glassware buyers attending the show. New techniques included the use of applied green trim to bowls, vases, ash trays and other shapes. The Bubble ball connector was used in eight new vases, one bowl and one compote. Bubble Optic made its appearance in a selection of ash trays and bowls. The Spiral Ball stem was used in the design of four vases in Twilight or Crystal. Twelve new vases were introduced featuring designs repeated from the January 3, 1952, Pittsburgh show, i.e. the 4-part Leaf stem and the 5 Rib Optic base. Other interesting items made for the show were a #60 Flip Vase with two 9" green streamers on the sides and a #1 14-oz. Old Fashion with two green handles and Bubble Optic.

Top left: Twilight #29, 12" Centerpiece Bowl, Bubble ball stem, Tiffin Optic. **$175-225**

Top right: Twilight #45, 12-1/4" h. Cupped Vase with Bubble ball stem, Tiffin Optic. **$175-225**

Bottom left: Twilight #31, 10" Heart Shape Bowl, Bubble Optic; #2 7" Ash Tray, Bubble Optic, both made offhand with one end curled up and the other end turned down. **$150-200; $125-150**

Next page:
Top: Crystal #4, 7-1/2" Ash Tray, 2 applied green streamers, Bubble Optic; Crystal #38, 7-1/2" Bowl, 3 green "leaves" cast on bottom of bowl to form base. **$115-140; $150-175**

Center: Crystal #2, 6" Bon Bon, with applied green streamer. **$115-140**

Bottom: Crystal #39, 12" Bowl, 3 applied green "leaves" cast on bowl to form base. **$150-175**

Right: Crystal #6416, 9-1/2" h. Dahlia Vase, Spiral Ball connector and 4 "leaves" cast onto bottom of vase, Tiffin Optic; #8, 10" Bowl, Spiral Ball connector and 4 "leaves" cast onto bottom of bowl, Tiffin Optic. **$150-175; $125-150**

Below: Detail of Spiral Ball Stem.

Above: Twilight #46, 11-1/4" h. Vase, Spiral Ball connector and 4 "leaves" cast onto bottom of vase, Tiffin Optic. **$250-300**

Pine #44, 16" Bowl, 7 parts turned under on rim of bowl. **$100-125**

January 8, 1953
Glass Trade Show

The Scallop Edge and the Bubble ball connector were the two main features of the fifty-five new glassware items exhibited at the January 8, 1953, glass trade show held in Pittsburgh. The Scallop Edge was a new design, while the Bubble ball was a carryover from the previous year's July show in New York City. Other successful lines repeated at this show were the Air Twist Stem, Bubble Optic, Manzoni Foot, and the 5 Rib Optic base.

Two #12 Center Peg Ash Trays in Twilight were displayed, one with Bubble Optic and one without optic. The popular Air Twist Stem was shown in Crystal on the #10 Crystal Compote, in green on the #11 and #13 Crystal Compotes and in green on the #75 Crystal Sweet Pea Vase.

Twilight #15, 8-1/4" h. "Teardrop" Bubble stem Candlestick, c. 1955. **$135-160**

Pine #8, 8" Ash Tray, made offhand with top turned down and under to form ring, 4 cigar rests, Bubble Optic. **$125-175**

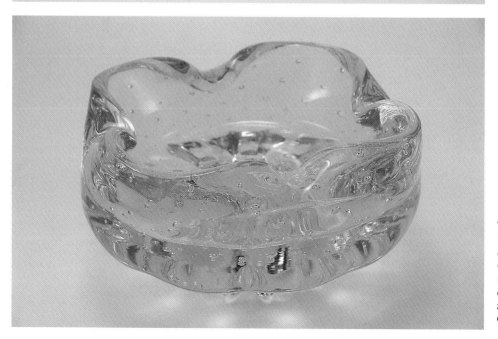

Twilight #10, 7-1/2" Ash Tray, 4 cigar rests, Bubble Optic. Same as #1 Ash Tray, except smaller and with Bubble Optic. **$200-250**

Twilight #4, 7" Bon Bon, heart shape, applied handle, Tiffin Optic. **$75-100**

Twilight #58, 8" "Scallop Edge" Bowl. **$250-300**

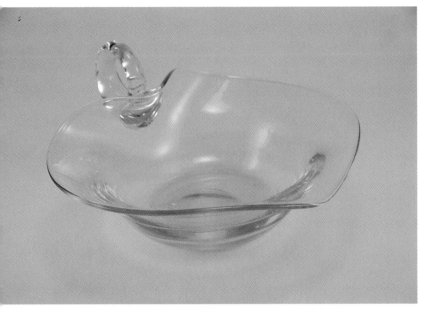

Twilight #58, 8" "Scallop Edge" Bowl. **$250-300**

Twilight #51, 5" h. "Scallop Edge" Rose Bowl, Bubble Optic. **$300-350**

Twilight #55, 12" "Scallop Edge" Center Bowl, 10 Rib Optic base. **$250-300**

Wistaria #1, 10-1/2" h. Hurricane Vase, Crystal applied foot, Tiffin Optic. **$275-325**

Top left: Crystal #14, 6" Compote, Pine offhand Air Twist stem, Tiffin Optic. **$150-200**

Center left: Detail of Pine Air Twist Stem.

Bottom left: Crystal #12, 4-1/2" Compote, Pine Bubble stem and foot. **$125-175**

Crystal #79, 10-1/4" h. Vase, applied Pine handle. **$150-200**

Twilight #77, 9-1/4" h. Vase with Manzoni foot, a heavy applied base with 4 curled cast toes. The vase is rectangular with rounded corners and concave sides. **$350-400**

July 19, 1953
Glass Trade Show

The new shapes chosen for the July 19, 1953, Glass Trade Show held in New York City included two epergnes, the #1 Cornucopia and four cigarette servers and boxes. Several new styles of bases were introduced; the paperweight Controlled Bubble base as seen on the #83 Lily Vase, a base similar to the #17430 foot with four pulled down toes, and a "Fin" base with three turned down toes. As in past shows, great emphasis was placed on vases, and they comprised one-fourth of the forty items offered. Of interest was the number of cigarette containers designed for the show. Crystal and Twilight remained the predominate colors.

Twilight #19, 6" Compote; the applied base consists of four toes with "knobs" protruding above and between each toe. **$100-125**

Twilight #86, 11" h. Flared Vase; #89, 10" h. Teardrop Vase, Tiffin Optic. **$250-300 each**

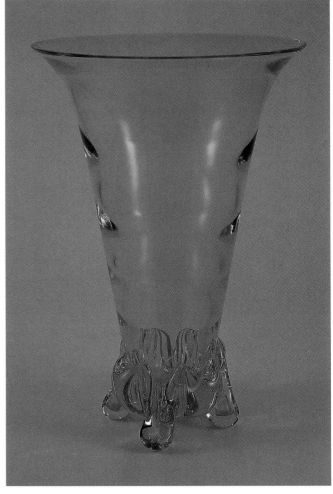

Twilight #86, 11" h. Flared Vase, Tiffin Optic. **$250-300**

Crystal #83, 16-1/2" h. Lily Vase, Controlled Bubble base (also made in Twilight). **$150-200**

Top left: Crystal #83, 11-1/4" h. Lily Vase, blown foot, Tiffin Optic. **$75-100**

Crystal #1, 10-1/4" h. Cornucopia, base 1-1/2" h., 10 Rib Optic, made offhand from spinner mold. **$225-275**

January 1954
Glass Trade Show

Only thirty-two pieces were exhibited at the January 1954 Glass Trade Show held in Pittsburgh, as compared to ninety items shown just two years earlier. However, the originality and creativity of the Tiffin Glassmasters was still evident in the innovative designs displayed at the 1954 show.

Examples shown: a group of tri-cornered bowls and vases; the #5411 Puritan line, which included the Cream, Sugar and 12" Bowl; the #5401 Drake Bowl; the #5400 Sleeping Duck Handled Ash Tray and Bon Bon; the #5402 Decanter with Crimped Ribbon (Rigaree) decoration; and two #5409 Vases with Crimped Ribbon decoration.

Top: Twilight #5401, 10" Drake Bowl. **$300-350**

Center: Wistaria #5400, 6" Bon Bon with Sleeping Duck handle. **$150-200**

Bottom: Twilight #5409, 11" d. Vase with crimped ribbon decoration. **$275-325**

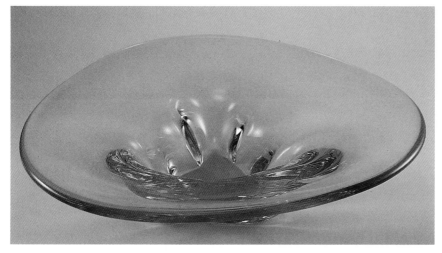

Twilight #5410, 12" Tri-Cornered Bowl, 3 Rib Optic. **$175-225**

Wistaria #5411, 4-1/2" across, Small Puritan Cream and Sugar, applied handles. **$200-250 set**

Twilight #5411, 4-1/2" across, Small Puritan Cream and Sugar. **$175-225**

Twilight #5411, 4-1/2" across, Large Puritan Sugar, applied Rainbow handle. **$100-125**

Chapter 17
Cuttings and Engravings

Decorative cuttings and engravings were applied to Tiffin's stemware from the early years until the closing of the factory in 1984. Production of other cut items occurred primarily from 1940-1950. After that date very few factory cuttings were produced. Individual cutters were allowed to design and cut pieces for their own use on their own time, and some of this glassware was signed by the artists. Production items were not signed.

Some of the skilled Tiffin cutters were: Willard Adams, John Bakies, Ardinelle Border, Al Brunner, Mabel Burnside, Beverly Collins, Irma Conn, Al Davies, Barney Derflinger, Mary Rose Deibert, Hubert Elchert, Jim Fowler, Alyce Bolander Goetz, William "Duke" Greiner, Bill Helterbran, Carl Henderson, Edna Henderson, Alyce Mae Hunker, Clyde King, Dave King, Pete Kirby, Eileen Loose, Carl Lovejoy, Jack Matthews, Don Morrow, Helen Reuter, Jack Reuter, Lester Shelton, Madelyn Strausser, John Van Horn and Fred Windstine.

Displayed in an exhibit of Tiffin Crystal in the early 1960s were the following: several Presentation Vases including the Crescent Bowl; #6402 Pheasants; #6553 Empress Flower Basket; #6600 Empress Bow Vase; and a selection of stemware. *Photo courtesy Seneca County Museum, Tiffin, Ohio.*

Left: Crystal #5859, 10" h. Flip Vase, miter cutting by William "Duke" Greiner, c. 1940s. **$250-300**

Below: Detail of side panel of vase.

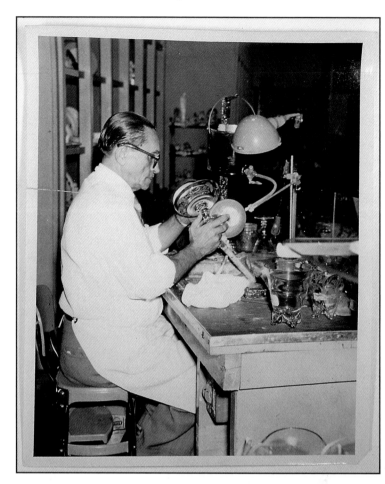

"Duke" Greiner, with #17430 Sweet Pea Vases on the work bench. *Photo courtesy Seneca County Museum, Tiffin, Ohio.*

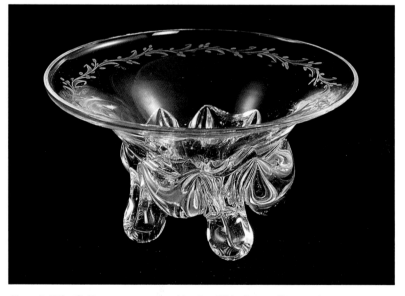

Crystal #19, 6" Compote, engraved by Fred Windstine. Also made in Citron, Copen Blue and Twilight. **$100-125**

Crystal, 9-1/4" h. Teardrop Vase, Strawberry Diamond and Fan miter cutting and faceted foot, unknown line number. Cut by Lester Shelton. **$275-325**

Opposite:
Crystal, 12" h. Vase, allover "Leaf and Floral" engraving, spiral cut Controlled Bubble ball connector, miter cut foot, unknown line number, engraved by Fred Windstine. **$500-700**

Detail of "Leaf and Floral" engraving.

Crystal, 10-1/2" h. Flared Vase. Reportedly, one of a pair of vases engraved with the likeness of President Dwight Eisenhower, the patriotic engraving includes Stars and the White House crest, c. 1955. **$1,000-1,500**

122

Left: Twilight, 6-3/4" h. Vase, allover facet cutting, unknown line number, c. 1951. **$250-300**

Below: Twilight, 12" h. Vase, "Leaf and Floral" engraving, Tiffin Optic, unknown line number. **$150-200**

Detail of "Bird" engraving.

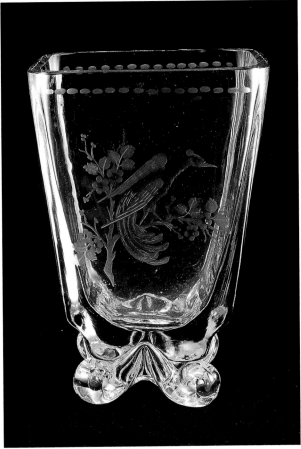

Crystal #6448, 9" h. Oblong Vase, "Bird" engraving and Manzoni foot, c. 1953. **$175-225**

123

Chapter 18

Cobalt Blue with "Opal Loops"

The Cobalt Blue with "Opal Loops" ware was produced c. 1942 for a brief period of time in a limited number of pieces. A 1942 *Crockery and Glass Journal* advertisement listed the #17350 Daisy Vase for sale at $5.00 each and the #17350 Tall Flared Vase for sale at $7.00 each. This line is one of the most coveted Tiffin Glass decorations.

Cobalt Blue #17350, 11-1/2" h. Daisy Vase, "Opal Loops," Crystal ball connector. **$450-550**

Left: Cobalt Blue #525, 6-1/2" h. Rose Bowl, "Opal Loops," applied offhand 3-ball foot. **$450-550**

Opposite: Cobalt Blue #17350, 9-1/2" h. Tub Vase, "Opal Loops" and Crystal ball connector. **$450-550**

Opposite:
Top left: Copen Blue #510, 7" h.
Bowl, Swedish Optic, Nude.
$400-500

Cobalt Blue #17350, 10" h. Teardrop Vases, "Opal
Loops" and Crystal ball connectors. **$450-550 each**

Cobalt Blue #17350, 7-1/4" h. Sweet Pea Vases, "Opal Loops"
and Crystal ball connectors. **$450-550 each**

126

Chapter 19
Sand Carved Glass

Production of Tiffin's Sand Carved decoration spanned the years 1941-1949, and was used extensively on several lines of vases, plates, bowls and other items. For this procedure, a pattern was cut into a rubber-like material which surrounded the glass object. A mini sand blaster was then used to cut or carve the design into the exposed glass. Most of Tiffin's sand carved work was done by women workers who were trained by supervisors Carl Rendlen and Mel Weininger. Among Tiffin's sand carved patterns were: Roses, Magnolia, Camellia, the Huntress, Diana, Lily of the Valley, Morning Glory, Calla Lily, several Nudes, Daisy, Peasant Girl, Rhododendron and Poppy.

Other artists, including Dorothy Thorpe, Franz Grosz and Billy Ray, decorated Tiffin blanks with their sand carved designs. Their signatures can be found on many of these pieces; the sand carvings from the Tiffin factory, however, were never signed. The predominant colors with sand carving are Crystal and Copen Blue, with other colors being rare.

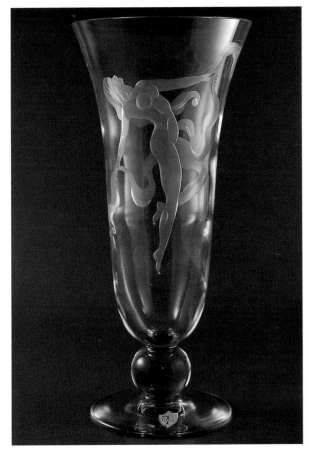

Crystal #17350, 12-3/4" h. Flared Vase, Swedish Optic, Nude. **$400-500**

Detail of Nude Sand Carving.

Crystal #5859, 14" h.
Flip Vase, Swedish
Optic, Peasant Girl.
$400-500

Detail of Peasant Girl Sand Carving.

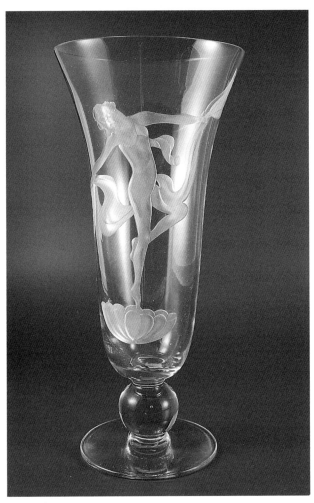

Crystal #17350, 12-3/4" h. Flared
Vase, Swedish Optic, Nude. **$400-500**

Opposite: Crystal #510, 7" h. Bowl, Swedish Optic, Nude. **$350-450**

Crystal #5961, 9" h. Jug, Bubble ball connector; #5811, 4-1/4" Cream and Sugar. Swedish Optic, Roses. **$150-200; $100-125 set**

Detail of the rosebud on the Roses Sand Carving.

Crystal #5855, 14" h. Vase,
Swedish Optic, Roses. **$150-200**

Crystal #17350, 9-1/2" h. Tub Vase; #17350 9" h. Globe Vase;
#5859, 10" h. Flip Vase. Swedish Optic, Roses. **$150-200;
$150-200; $125-175**

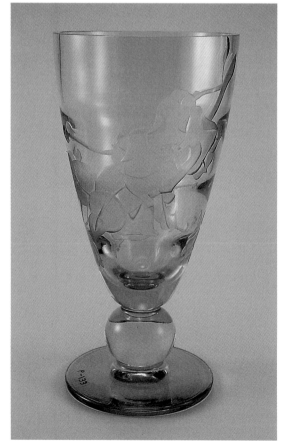

Copen Blue #17350, 7" h. Sweet Pea Vases, Crystal ball connectors,
Swedish Optic, Roses. **$175-200 each**

Copen Blue #17350, 10" h. Teardrop Vase, Crystal ball
connector, Swedish Optic, Magnolia. **$175-200**

Crystal #17350, 12-3/4" h.
Flared Vase; #5920, 8" h.
Blown Rectangular Vase.
Swedish Optic, Roses.
$150-200; $125-175

Two types of Roses were
used in Tiffin's sand
carvings, one a rosebud,
the other an open petal
rose. This is the detail for
the open petal rose motif.

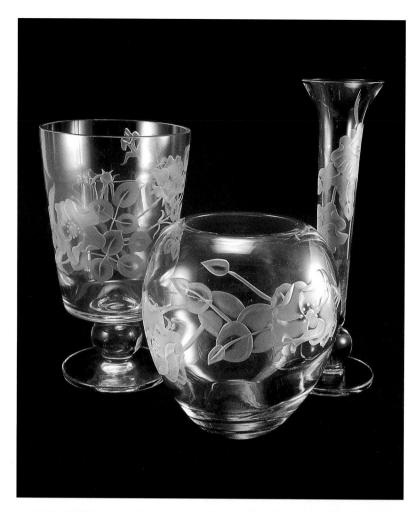

Left: Crystal #17350, 9" h. Tub Vase; #510 7" h. Bowl; #17350, 10-1/2" h. Bud Vase. Swedish Optic Roses. **$150-200; $125-175; $150-200**

Below: Crystal #17350, 11-1/2" h. Urn Vase; #17350, 7-1/4" h. Sweet Pea Vase; #17350, 8" h. Center Bowl. Swedish Optic, Roses. **$150-200 each**

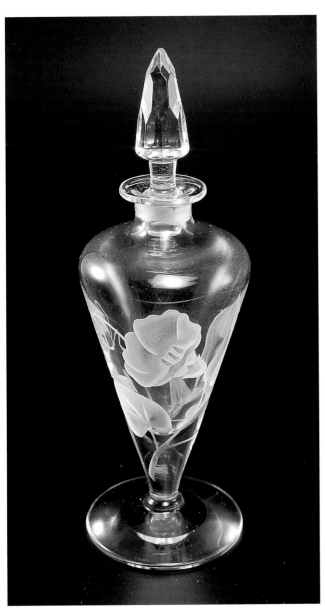

Crystal, 8-1/2" h. Cologne, faceted stopper, unknown line number, sand carving with tinted petals. $75-100

Close-up of tinted petals.

Left: Copen Blue #5920, 10" h. Blown Rectangular Vase, Swedish Optic, "Mallard Duck" sand carving. **$175-225**

Below: Detail of "Mallard Duck" sand carving.

Top left: Crystal #101, 11" h. Vase, "Wavy" Optic, Cross. **$125-175**

Top right: Copen Blue #5859, 10" h. Flip Vase; #17350, 10" h. Teardrop Vase. Crystal ball connector, Swedish Optic, Magnolia. **$150-200; $175-225**

Left: Crystal #17350, 7" h. Compote; #17350, 10-1/4" h. Fan Vase. Swedish Optic, Magnolia. **$125-175; $150-200**

Crystal #17350, 12-3/4" h. Flared Vase, Swedish Optic, Magnolia. **$150-200**

Detail of Magnolia sand carving.

Opposite:

Top left: Crystal #102, 15" h. Vase, Magnolia. **$150-200**

Top right: Crystal #101, 12" h. Vase, Swedish Optic, Calla Lily. **$150-200**

Bottom left: Crystal #5859, 11-1/2" h. Flip Vase, Camellia. **$150-200**

Bottom right: Wistaria #17523, 13" h. Flared Vase, Crystal Cellini stem and foot, Tiffin Optic, Morning Glory. **$325-375**

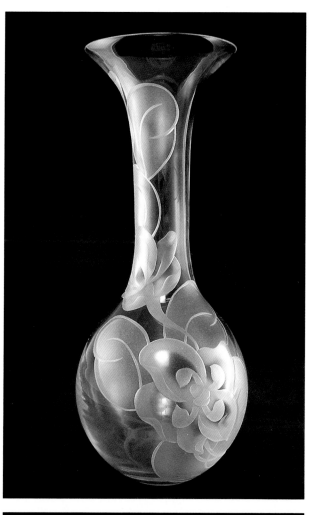

Chapter 20
Ruby and Cranberry Stained Glass

Ruby or Cranberry stain was applied to Crystal blanks prior to firing. A November 1942 advertisement from *Crockery and Glass Journal* states that seven different graceful shapes were available at prices ranging from $5.00 to $10.00 retail. Some of the stained ware was decorated with attractive engravings. Since stained pieces scratched easily, unblemished examples are hard to find today.

Crystal with Ruby Stain #17350, 11-1/2" h. Daisy Vase; Crystal with Cranberry Stain #17350, 9-1/2" h. Teardrop Vase. Swedish Optic. **$65-90 each**

Left: Crystal with Ruby Stain #17350, 11-1/2" h. Daisy Vase; #17350, 9-1/2" h. Tub Vase. Swedish Optic. **$65-90 each**

Below: Crystal with Ruby Stain #8833, 8" Plate, sand carved Roses; #17350, 10" h. Teardrop Vase, sand carved Roses. **$50-75; $150-200**

Above: Crystal with Ruby Stain #17350, 9" Fruit Bowl, faceted ball stem, Parkwood engraving. **$125-150**

Right: Crystal with Ruby Stain #17350, 12-3/4" h. Flared Vase., "Bird" engraving by "Duke" Greiner, c. 1942. **$175-225**

Next Page: Detail of "Bird" motif engraving.

141

Chapter 21
Gold Encrustations & Enameling

In the 1940s Tiffin decorated a large number of shapes in Crystal, Opal, Copen Blue and Killarney with gold encrustations. The Rose of Britain and Melrose etchings were the two most popular designs used with this decoration. Gold was also used extensively to decorate many stemware patterns throughout Tiffin's production years.

The use of enamel decoration was common in the 1920-1930 era; however, this treatment is considered unusual for the later years.

Copen Blue #101, 12" h. Vase, gold-filled "Rose" engraving, Swedish Optic, c. 1940. **$75-100**

Detail of gold-filled "Rose" engraving.

Above: Crystal #5859, 10" h. Flip Vase; #510 7" h. Bowl; #17350 10" h. Teardrop Vase. Swedish Optic, gold encrusted Rose of Britain etching, c. 1945. **$125-150; $125-150; $150-175**

Crystal #5859, 10" h. Flip Vase; #17350, 12-3/4" h. Flared Vase. Swedish Optic, gold encrusted Rose of Britain etching, c. 1945. **$125-150; $150-175**

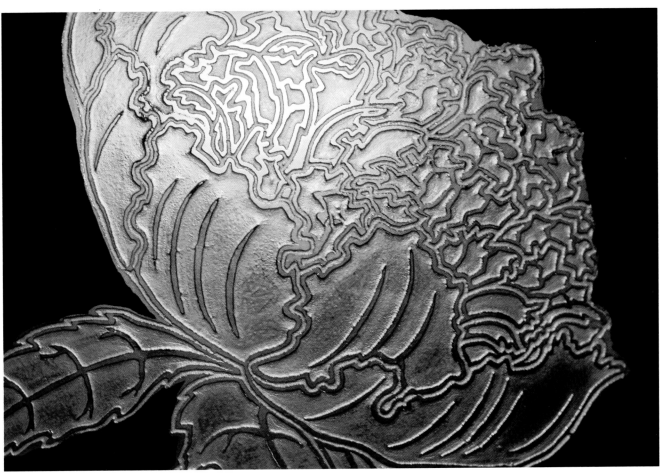

Top: Killarney #17430, 7-1/2" h. Flared Vase; 6" h. Sweet Pea Vase, applied Crystal feet, gold encrusted Rose of Britain etching, c. 1948.
$175-225 each

Above: Detail of gold encrusted Rose of Britain etching.

Crystal #17350, 9-1/4" h. Tub Vase, gold encrusted Springtime etching, c. 1945. **$150-200**

Close-up of Springtime etching.

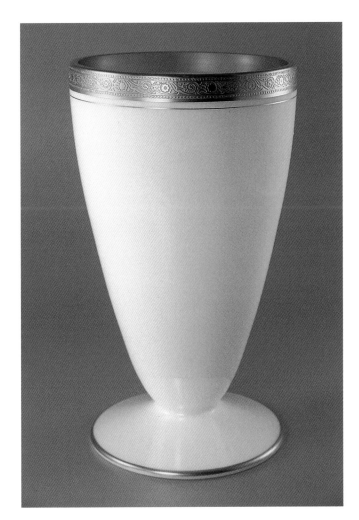

Right: Opal #5856, 8-1/2" h.
Teardrop Vase, gold encrusted
Minton band, c. 1942. **$200-250**

Below: Detail of gold encrusted
Minton band.

Killarney #17430, 7-1/2" h. Flared Vase, applied Crystal foot, gold encrusted Melrose Green etching and band. **$175-225**

Opposite: Killarney #6037 4" Candleholder, applied Crystal trim; #17430, 10" h. Daisy Vase; #17430, 6-1/4" Compote. Gold encrusted Melrose Green etching and band. **$75-100; $175-225; $100-125**

Detail of gold encrusted Melrose Green etching and band.

Killarney advertisement from a 1949 issue of *Crockery and Glass Journal*.

Opposite: Killarney #17430, 10-1/4" h.
Urn Vase, applied Crystal foot, gold
encrusted Bouquet Green etching and
Laurel band. **$175-225**

Opposite: Killarney #6118, 10" h. Bud Vases, Crystal feet. The bud vase on the left is decorated in a hand painted gold leaf design as shown in a department store advertisement by Abels, Wasserberg and Co. The decorator is identified as Charleton in the January 1949 issue of *Crockery and Glass Journal*. This decorated line was available in eighteen different shapes. The bud vase on the right has gold and enamel decoration. **$65-90 each**

Killarney #17430, 6" h. Sweet Pea Vase, applied Crystal foot, gold encrusted Bouquet Green etching and Laurel band. **$150-200**

Detail of gold encrustation on Bouquet Green etching and Laurel band.

Killarney with Crystal trim, #6037, 4" candleholders with "Grapevine" gold and enamel decoration, 1949. **$125-150 pair**

Killarney #17430, 6-1/2" Rose Bowl with applied Crystal foot and "Grapevine" gold and enamel decoration, 1949. **$125-150**

Detail of "Grapevine."

154

Chapter 22
Craquelle (Crackle) Glass

Craquelle pieces were created by immersing the hot glass object in water. This ware is only known in Crystal in the #17430 line. Very limited production occurred in the 1950s.

Crystal #17430, 6" h. Rose Bowl; #17430 6" h. Sweet Pea Vase with Craquelle decoration. **$150-200 each**

Chapter 23
Mica

In the early 1950s Tiffin produced a line of cased glass-ware embedded with mica flakes. Several known Tiffin shapes were included, however, many unfamiliar designs were also utilized. Pine is the predominant color used in this line. All Mica pieces are considered rare.

Pine, 9-1/4" h. Vase, Crystal foot, unknown line number. **$250-300**

Pine, 11-1/2" Tri-cornered Bowl, unknown line number. **$250-300**

Right: Pine, 10-1/4" h. Vase; 9-1/4" h. Vase with Crystal foot. Unknown line numbers. **$250-300 each**

Below: Pine, 10-1/4" h. Vases, unknown line numbers. **$250-300 each**

Above: Pine, 12" Shallow Bowl, unknown line number. **$200-250**

Left: Pine, 14" h. Vase, 5 Rib Optic, unknown line number. **$275-325**

Right: Pine, 12-1/2" h. Jugs, Pine and Crystal applied handles, unknown line number. The sides of the jugs have a flattened appearance. **$375-425 each**

Below: Pine #5508, 12" Cornucopia, applied Crystal feet. **$325-375**

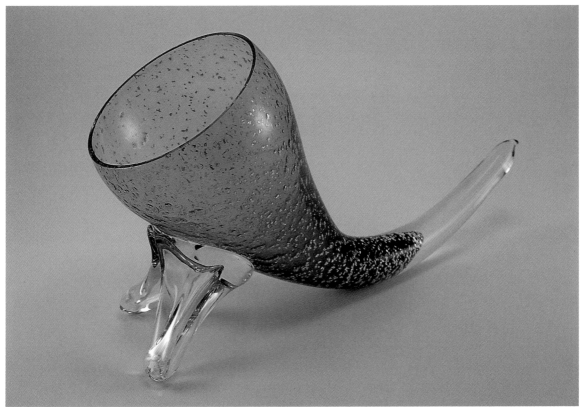

Pine, 7" h. Flared Vase; 8" h.
Cupped Vase, unknown line
numbers. **$250-300 each**

Pine #96, 18" h. Vases.
$250-300 each

Right: Rose Blush #5513, 10-3/4" h. Tri-Panel Vase.
$200-250

Below: Detail of original factory sticker showing line number 96 and a price of $5.20.

Amberina #17430, 6-3/8" Compote, applied Crystal foot. **$200-250**

Chapter 24
"Ribbon"

A colored ribbon was applied to the "Ribbon" ware after it was removed from the spinner mold. The piece was then reinserted into the mold, pressing the ribbon into the molded ribs. The colors used in the "Ribbon" line were Green Fantasy, Ruby Fantasy, Wild Rose, Rose Blush, Cerulean, and Azure. Green Fantasy and Ruby Fantasy are combinations of Green and Crystal and Ruby and Crystal respectively; the others are solid colors. All of the colors were listed in a 1956 catalog, except Ruby Fantasy, which was in a 1960 price list.

Green Fantasy #5529, 14" Oval Bowl, 10 Rib Optic. **$175-225**

Green Fantasy, 15-1/2" h. Vase, 10 Rib Optic, unknown line number. **$225-275**

Green Fantasy #5532, 13-1/2" h. Plate, 10 Rib Optic. **$175-225**

Green Fantasy, #5528, 12" Flared Bowl, 10 Rib Optic. **$225-275**

Green Fantasy, 17" h. Vase, 10 Rib Optic, unknown line number. **$175-225**

Green Fantasy #5538, 8-1/2" h.
Vase, 10 Rib Optic. **$225-275**

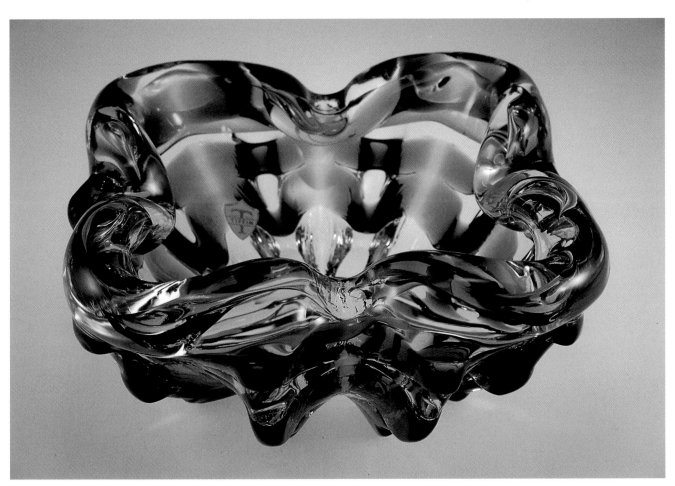

Green Fantasy, 12" Crimped Bowl, 10 Rib Optic, unknown line number. **$225-275**

Top: Green Fantasy #5528, 8" Ash Tray, 10 Rib Optic. **$225-275**

Green Fantasy #5526,
11-1/2" h. Crimped
Vase, 10 Rib Optic.
$225-275

Detail of Green Fantasy Vase.

Green Fantasy #5527,
21-1/2" h. Vase, 10 Rib
Optic. **$175-225**

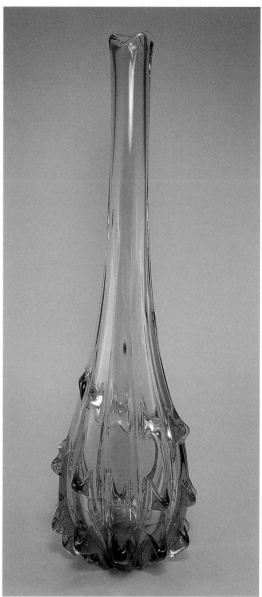

Above: Wild Rose #5577, 19" h. Vase, 10 Rib Optic. **$125-150**

Top left: Wild Rose #5529, 15" Oval Bowl, 10 Rib Optic. **$125-150**

Center left: Rose Blush #5530, 9" Ash Tray, 10 Rib Optic. **$125-150**

Bottom left: Cerulean #5529, 14" Oval Bowl, 10 Rib Optic. **$125-150**

Wild Rose #5530, 9" Ash Tray, 10 Rib Optic. **$125-150**

Top: Wild Rose, #5534, 14" Gardenia Bowl, 10 Rib Optic. **$125-150**

Chapter 25
Satin Glass

During the 1920s and 1930s, satin glass was produced in vast amounts by the U.S. Glass Company. The popularity of satin glass waned and was rarely included in Tiffin's inventory after that time. In the early 1970s an attempt was made to reproduce the satin finish; however, this proved unsuccessful, and only a minimal number of Modern items were produced.

Right: Copen Blue #17350, 10" h. Flared Vase, geometric engraving, c. 1940. **$125-150**

Below: Twilight #6555, 10" h. Flared Vase; #5461, 9" Oval Bowl, 10 Rib Optic, c. 1970. **$125-175 each**

Desert Red #17430, 8" Centerpiece Bowl, applied foot, Tiffin Optic, c. 1965. **$40-65**

Opposite:

Top: Persimmon #6550, 14" Flower Bowl, c. 1970. **$65-90**

Bottom: Persimmon #6576, 7" h. Large Rose Bowl, c. 1970. **$65-90**

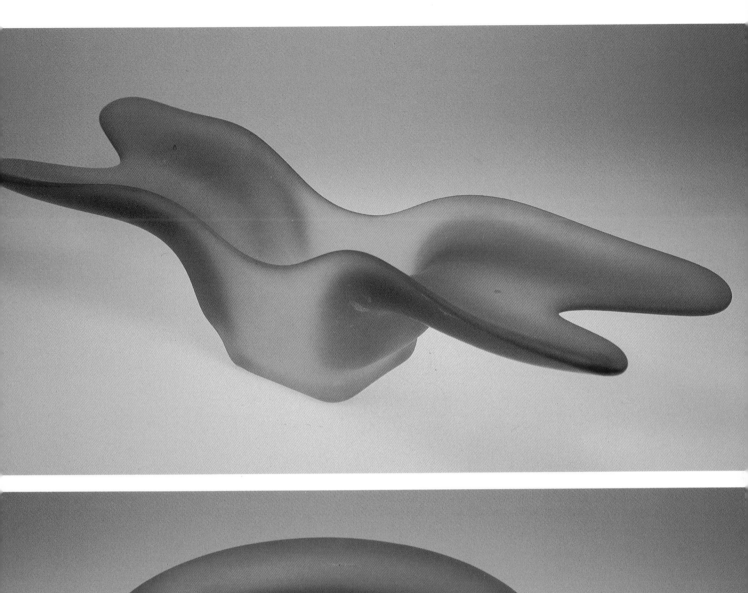

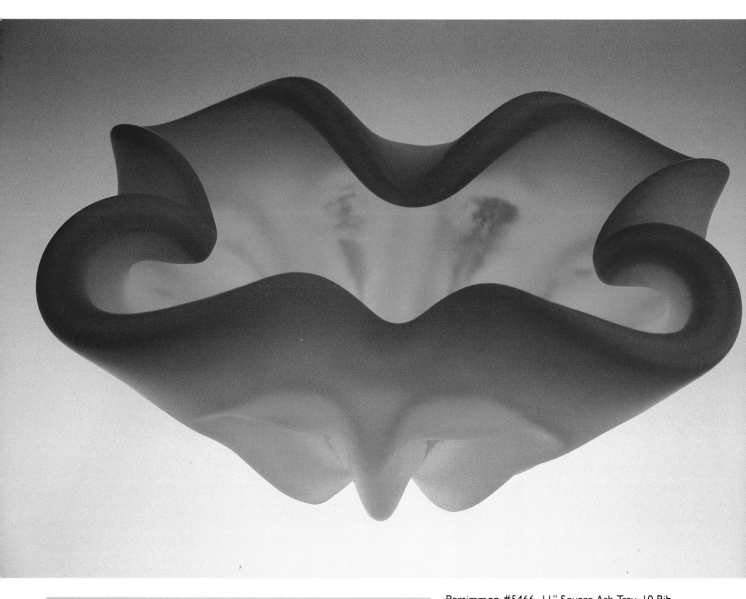

Persimmon #5466, 11" Square Ash Tray, 10 Rib Optic. **$65-90**

Empire Green 8" Bowl, 10 Rib Optic, unknown line number, c. 1970. **$40-65**

Chapter 26
Controlled Bubble and Bubble Stem

The Controlled Bubble decoration was used primarily on the #17350 line in the 1940s and should not be confused with Bubble Optic. Attractive Controlled Bubble ball connectors in Ruby, Copen Blue and Amber enhanced vases and bowls produced in this line. The Controlled Bubble ball decoration was also used for the Crystal foot on the #5987 Vase, #83 Lily Vase and the #6301 and #6302 Cornucopias.

The Bubble stem was developed by Paul Williams and was used in the 1940s and early 1950s in the production of vases, bowls and candleholders in several different lines. Known colors are Crystal, Copen Blue, Wistaria and Twilight.

In 1961, "Tiffin Selections," a company pamphlet, also illustrated several items produced with the Bubble stem. These pieces are documented in the colors of Plum, Golden Banana, Cobalt Blue and Empire Green.

Copen Blue #17350, 9" h. Fruit Bowl, Crystal foot, Crystal with Ruby Controlled Bubble "paperweight" connector, Swedish Optic. **$250-300**

Crystal #17350, 12-3/4" h. Flared Vase; Crystal #17350 9"
h. Flared Vase with Ruby Controlled Bubble ball connectors,
Swedish Optic. **$200-250 each**

Crystal #17350, 12-3/4" h. Flared Vase; Crystal #17350, 9"
h. Flared Vase, Amber Controlled Bubble ball connectors,
Swedish Optic. **$175-200 each**

Top left: Crystal, 13-3/4" h. Flared Vase, Controlled Bubble ball connector, Swedish Optic, unknown line number. **$125-150**

Top right: Crystal #5987, 11" h. Vase, offhand Controlled Bubble 3-ball foot, Swedish Optic, c. 1940. **$125-150**

Left: Crystal #17350, 9-1/4" h. Teardrop Vase, Controlled Bubble ball connector; Crystal #17350 6-1/2" h. Vase, engraved "Best Puppy, Evanger." Swedish Optic. **$125-150; $65-85**

Opposite Top: Crystal #17350, 9" h. Flared Vases with Amber, Copen Blue, and Ruby Controlled Bubble ball connectors, Swedish Optic. **$175-200; $175-200; $200-225**

Above: 1961 "Tiffin Selections" Pamphlet.

Left: 1961 "Tiffin Selections" Pamphlet.

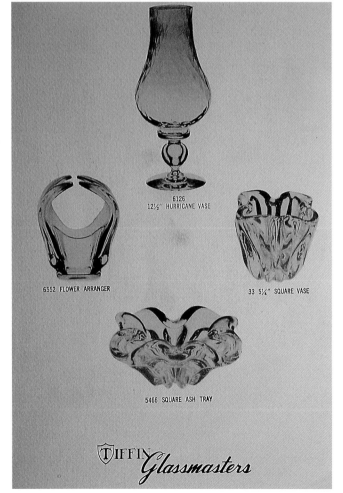

Opposite: Crystal #17383, 7-1/4" h. Sweet Pea Vase, Orange, Blue and White stripes, Bubble ball connector, experimental piece, c. 1940.
$175-225

176

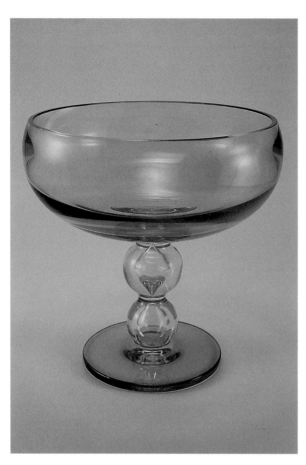

Copen Blue #583, 9" h. Bowl, offhand Crystal Bubble stem, Swedish Optic, c. 1940. **$125-150**

Crystal, 14" Centerpiece Bowl, "Teardrop" Bubble base, unknown line number. **$100-125**

Crystal, 7" h. Vase, off hand, "Teardrop" Bubble in heavy sham base, applied handles, unknown line number; Crystal #15, 8-1/4" h. Candlestick, "Teardrop" Bubble stem, c. 1955. **$175-200; $75-100**

Copen Blue #554, 8" h. Bowl, offhand Crystal Bubble 2-ball stem, Swedish Optic, c. 1940. **$125-150**

Top left: Crystal, 9-3/4" h. Cruet, "Teardrop" Bubble base, applied handle and stopper, unknown line number. **$100-125**

Top right: Cobalt Blue with Crystal trim #6131, 14" h. Vase, Bubble ball stem, c. 1961. **$225-275**

Left: Cobalt Blue with Crystal Trim #6132, 8" h. Rose Bowl, Bubble ball stem, c. 1961. **$225-275**

Top left: Plum #6127, 9-1/2" Centerpiece Bowl, Bubble ball stem, c. 1961. **$150-175**

Top right: Plum #6126, 12-1/2" h. Hurricane Vase, Bubble ball stem, Diamond Optic, c. 1961. Shade is attached to candleholder. **$225-275**

Left: Golden Banana #6111, 5-1/4" Compote; Golden Banana #6133, 12" h. Vase with Diamond Optic, Bubble ball stems, c. 1961. **$100-125; $150-200**

Opposite: Crystal, 9-1/2" x 11" h., "Crescent" Bowl, Bubble stem and "Leaf" engraving, unknown line number, c. 1962. **$!,000-1,500**

Chapter 27
Presentation Vases

Presentation vases were awarded for special achievement to workers or visiting dignitaries. Beautiful miter cuttings or engravings enhanced Crystal vases produced for these special occasions. One of the outstanding features of the presentation vases was the thick, heavy base to which miter cuttings were often applied. The name of the honoree, the date and other significant information were cut on the body of the vase.

Crystal, 8-1/4" h. Flared Vase, 2" thick base, miter cutting, Tiffin Optic, unknown line number, c. 1962. **$175-225**

Crystal #6316, 9" h. Flared Vase, 2" thick miter cut base, Tiffin Optic, c. 1955. **$150-200**

Crystal, 9" h. Flared Vase, 2" thick base, Tiffin Optic, unknown line number, c. 1962. **$125-175**

Crystal, 10" h. Flared Vase, heavy base, Tiffin Optic, unknown line number, c. 1962. **$125-175**

Chapter 28
Square Foot Vases

The square foot was used on stemware blanks, which Tiffin produced for the Hawkes cuttings. Use of the square foot on vases was not common and few examples are found.

Crystal, 11/12" h. Square Foot Urn Vase, ball connector, unknown line number. **$150-200**

Crystal #6088, 10-1/2" h. Square Foot Vase, Tiffin Optic. **$125-150**

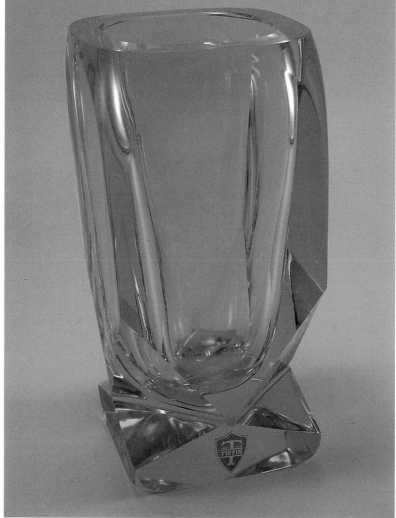

Left: Twilight, 8" h. Square Vase, faceted corners and foot, unknown line number. Probably a non-production item. **$250-300**

Opposite: Wistaria #6088, 7-1/2" h. Square Foot Vase, Tiffin Optic, c. 1950. **$325-400**

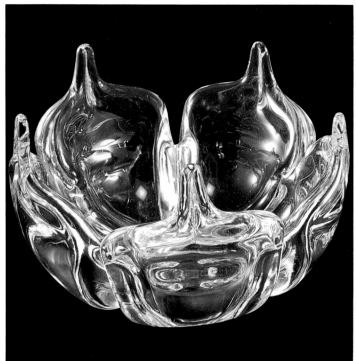

Chapter 29
Free Form Shapes

Many of the products of Tiffin's Modern era were large freeform shapes which required the special skills of the blowers and finishers. Great strength and dexterity were needed to shape the heavy molten glass into beautiful creations by the Tiffin Glassmasters. Among the artists who deserve recognition are: Oscar Theller, Vincent Meier, Archie Kahler, Mr. Tucker, Hugo Wahl, Arthur Widegren, Johnny Slottermiller, Johnny Fleming, Paul Hoover, Eric Theller and Al Krupp.

Top: Wistaria and Twilight #5451, 4-1/2" Narcissus Bowls. **$200-250; $175-225**

Above: Crystal #5451, 6" Narcissus Bowl. **$50-75**

Twilight, 15" Free Form Bowl, unknown line number. **$150-200**

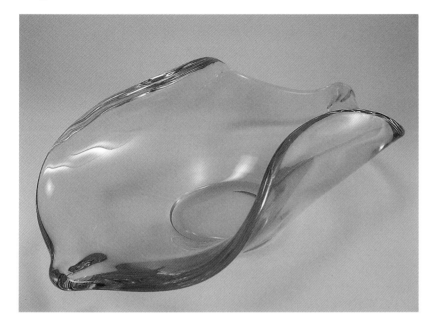

Twilight #5463, 13" Bowl, c. 1955. **$125-150**

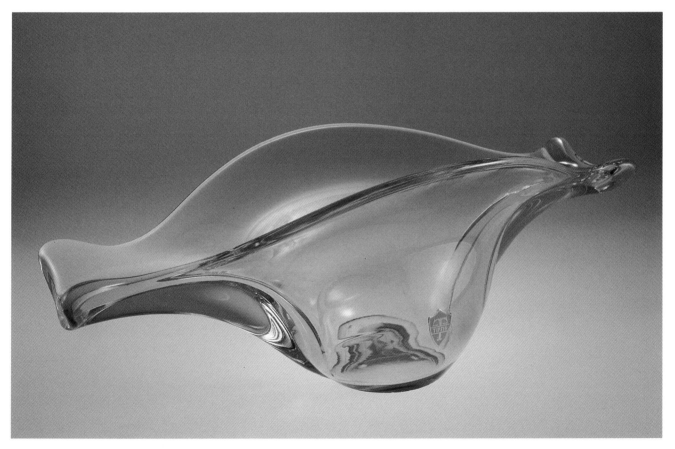

Twilight #6613, 16" T.V. Bowl, c. 1955. **$150-175**

Crystal #17424, 16" h. Free Form
Vase, c. 1965. **$50-75**

Copen Blue #17424, 16" h. Free Form
Vase, c. 1965. **$75-100**

Greenbriar #17424, 16" h. Free Form
Vase, c. 1967. **$40-65**

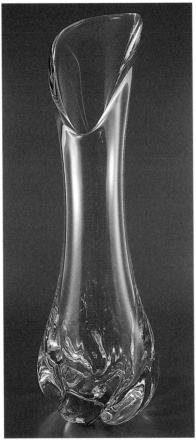

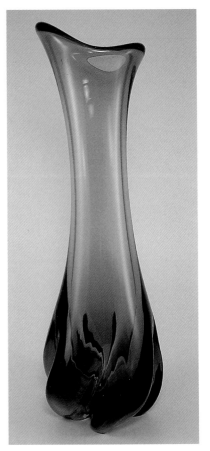

Greenbriar, 13" Shallow Bowl, 4 crimped sides, unknown
line number, c. 1967. **$40-65**

Opposite: Persimmon #17424, 14-1/2" h. Free Form Vase, with
Opalescence; #6577, 20" h. Vase, with Opalescence. **$75-100 each**

Chapter 30
Ash Trays

Twilight #5466, 11" Square Ash Tray, 4 cigar rests, 10 Rib Optic. **$150-200**

Golden Banana #5466, 11" Square Ash Tray, 4 cigar rests, 10 Rib Optic, c. 1961. **$100-125**

Twilight #5453, 10" Heart Shape Ash Tray, 10 Rib Optic. **$150-200**

Copen Blue, 8-1/2" Ash Tray, unknown line number. **$50-75**

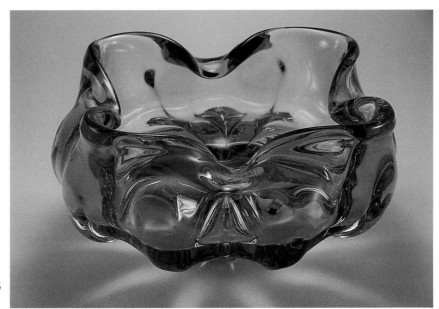

Copen Blue #1, 8" Ash Tray, 4 cigar rests, 10 Rib Optic, c. 1965. **$125-175**

Greenbriar #5, 8-1/2" Ash Tray, rolled under rim, c. 1967. **$40-65**

Chapter 31
Bon Bons and Nappies

Wistaria, 6-1/4" Nappy, applied handle, Tiffin Optic, unknown line number. **$90-115**

Top right: Killarney #6233, 6-1/2" Bon Bon; #6390, 6-1/2" Oval Bowl, applied Crystal handles, c. 1948. **$50-75 each**

Left: Wistaria #6281, 8" Bon Bon, applied handle, Tiffin Optic; 5" Bon Bon, applied handle, Tiffin Optic, unknown line number. **$90-115 each**

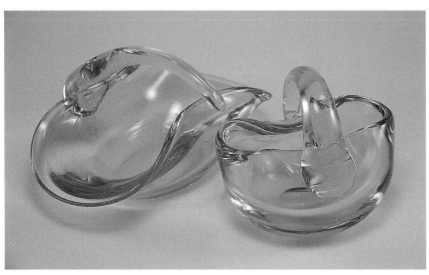

Twilight #5520 8" Nut Bowl, applied handle; #5411, 4-1/2" Large Puritan Sugar. **$125-150; $100-125.**

Twilight #5480, 6-3/4" Bon Bon, applied handle; Wistaria #6261, 7-1/2" Mint, applied handle. **$100-125; $90-115**

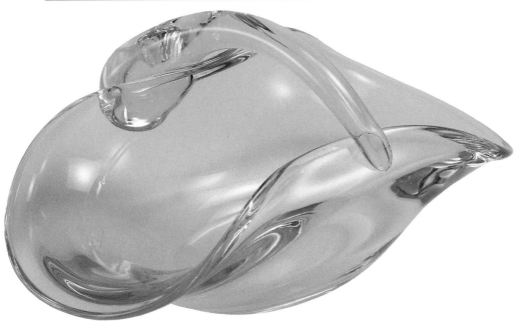

Above: Twilight #5520, 8" Nut Bowl, applied handle (a larger 11" bowl with applied Rainbow handle was also made). **$125-150**

Right: Crystal #6467, 5" Olive Dish, Tiffin Optic (also known in Citron Green and Copen Blue). **$40-65**

Killarney and Crystal #6364, 3" Candleholders, c. 1948; #6037 4" Candleholders, c. 1948. **$100-125 each pair**

Top: Copen Blue, 4" h. Candleholder, unknown line number; Copen Blue #17350, 4" h. Candleholders with Crystal ball connectors. **$45-65; $55-75 each**

Wistaria, 3-1/2" h. Candleholders, unknown line number; #17394, 4" h. Candleholders, Crystal foot. **$175-225 pair; $150-200 pair**

Top: Wistaria #17, 5" h. Candleholders, c 1950; #6037 4" h. Candleholders, c. 1950. **$175-225 each pair**

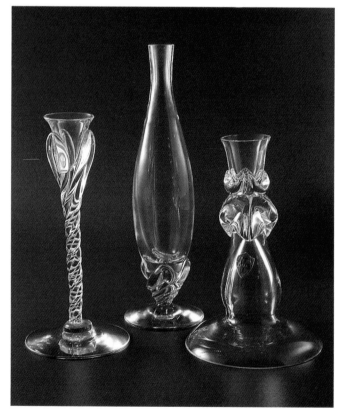

Cellini: Crystal, 5-1/4" h. Candleholder, unknown line number, c. 1947; 7" h. Candleholder, unknown line number, c. 1947; #17423, 6-1/4" h. Candleholder, c. 1965. **$100-125 each**

Crystal, 7-3/4" h. Candleholder, heavily twisted stem; 9-1/2"" h. "3Leaf Stem" Cordial Decanter; 7" h. Candleholder, blown foot, unknown line numbers. **$100-125 each**

Top: Wistaria and Crystal #6361, 5-1/4" h. Candleholders, Bubble stem, c. 1950. **$175-225 pair**

Opposite: Crystal #6460, 13-1/2" h. Candlesticks, twisted columns and button connectors, c. 1952. **$175-225 each**

Crystal #6420, 10" h. Candlesticks, c. 1952. **$175-225 each**

Twilight, 10" h. Candlestick; 8-1/2" h. Candlestick with Blown feet, Tiffin Optic, unknown line numbers; 4-1/2" h. Candleholders, unknown line number. **$200-250; $200-250; $150-175 pair**

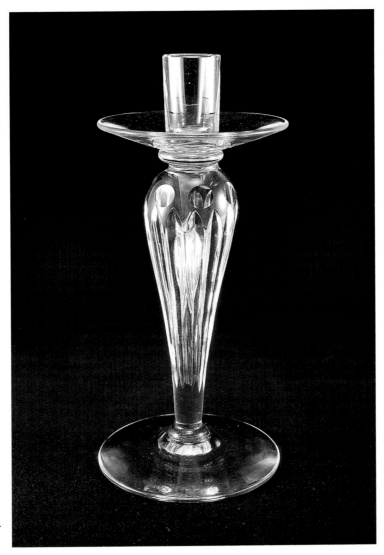

Crystal "Teardrop" 9-1/2"
Bubble stem candlestick,
unknown line number, c. 1955.
$150-200.

Twilight, 3-1/2" h. Candleholders, unknown line number;
#17, 5" h. Candleholders, c. 1954. **$150-175 pair;**
$150-200 pair

Twilight #6037, 4" h. Candleholders. **$150-175 pair**

Chapter 33
Candy Boxes

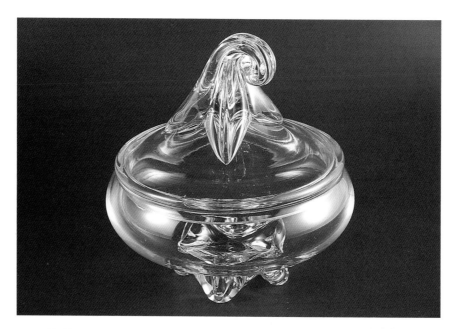

Crystal #6455, 6"
Candy Box, applied
foot and finial, c. 1955
(also known in Twilight).
$150-175

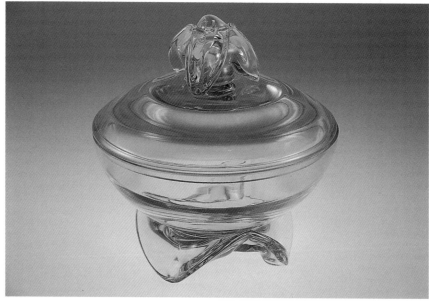

Twilight, 6-3/4" h.
Covered Candy Box,
applied "3 Fin foot,"
applied Crown finial,
Tiffin Optic, unknown
line number, c. 1954.
$225-275

Chapter 34
Compotes

Crystal, 7" Compote, blue offhand Air Twist ring stem, Tiffin Optic, unknown line number, c. 1952. **$150-200**

Detail of blue Air Twist ring stem.

Crystal, 5" "twist stem" Compote. The stem is the same as the #6460 candlesticks. **$75-100**

Twilight #6447, 6" Compote, Tiffin Optic, c. 1953. **$125-150**

Chapter 35
Cornucopias

Left: Copen Blue #5508, 15-1/2" Cornucopia, applied Crystal feet, c. 1965. **$125-175**

Below: Citron Green #5520, 8" Nut Bowl, applied handle; #5508, 13" Cornucopia, applied feet, c. 1965. **$50-75; $125-150**

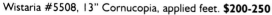

Wistaria #5508, 13" Cornucopia, applied feet. **$200-250**

Cerulean #5508, 12-1/2" Cornucopia, applied feet, c. 1956; #5507, 8" Cornucopia, applied feet, c. 1956. (This style of cornucopia was also produced in Twilight, Crystal, and Wild Rose). **$150-200; $125-150**

Crystal #6041 16-1/2"
Cornucopia, applied feet, Spiral
Optic. Many of the #6041
cornucopias were hand-
fashioned by glass workers John
Fleming and Paul Hoover. **$75-
100**

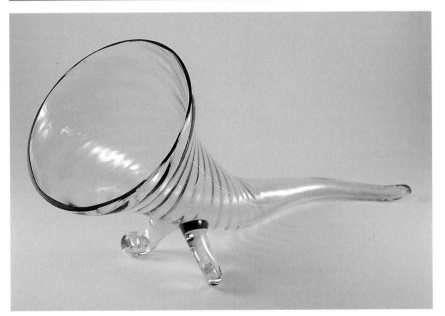

Copen Blue #6041, 16-1/2"
Cornucopia, applied Crystal
feet, Spiral Optic. **$100-125**

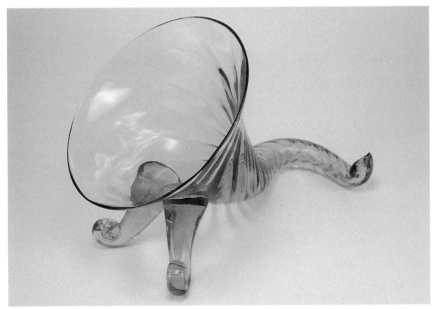

Wistaria #6041, 12" Cornucopia, applied feet, Spiral Optic,
c. 1950. **$325-375**

Twilight, Wistaria
#6041, 12" Cornuco-
pias, applied feet, Spiral
Optic, c. 1950. **$200-
250; $325-375**

Killarney #6041, 9-1/2" Cornucopia, applied Crystal feet, Spiral
Optic, c. 1950. **$200-250**

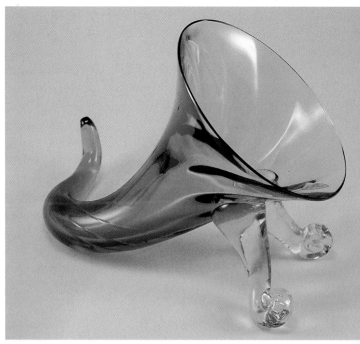

Citron Green #6041, 10" Cornucopia, applied feet, Spiral Optic, c. 1965. **$125-150**

Greenbriar #6041, 10" Cornucopia, applied Crystal feet, Spiral Optic, c. 1967. **$125-150**

Twilight #1, 10-1/2" h. Cornucopias, 10 Rib Optic, c. 1953. **$300-350 each**

Crystal #5919-A, 7" Cornucopias, Swedish Optic. Information from the September 1941 edition of *Crockery and Glass Journal* states that these retailed for $4.00 each. **$75-100 each**

Top left: Crystal #5983, 12-1/4" h. Cornucopia Vase, Half-Spiral Optic, Controlled Bubble connector, c. 1940. **$175-225**
Top right: Crystal #5919-B, 7-3/4" h. Cornucopia Vases, Swedish Optic, c. 1940. **$75-100 each**

Crystal #6302, 8" h. Cornucopia Vase, crimped rim, Controlled Bubble base, c. 1950. **$100-125**

Killarney #6302, 8" h. Cornucopia Vase, crimped rim, Crystal Controlled Bubble base. Also made in Wistaria, c. 1948. **$225-275**

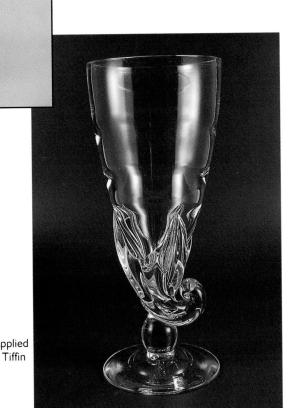

Crystal #6443, 11-1/4" h. Vase, applied "tail" joins vase to ball connector, Tiffin Optic, c. 1950. **$250-300**

Crystal #6409-A, 11-1/2" h. epergne. Vase fits into opening in footed bowl. Tiffin Optic, c. 1955. **$150-200**

Crystal #6464, 12" h. epergne. The epergnes were used for floral and/or fruit decorations, c. 1955. **$150-200**

Crystal #6409, 14" h. epergne, c. 1955. The vase removes from the bowl. **$150-200**

Chapter 37
Rose Bowls

Copen Blue #526, 4-1/4" h. Rose
Bowl, Kosta Optic, c. 1940 (also
made in 5-1/2" and 7" sizes).
$25-50

Copen Blue #525 6-3/4"
h., 4-1/2" h., 5-1/2" h.
Rose bowls, Crystal
offhand 3-ball feet,
Swedish Optic, c. early
1940s. **$65-90; $50-75;
$50-75**

Killarney #17430, 6-1/4" h.
Large Rose Bowl; 4-1/2" h.
Small Rose Bowl with
applied Crystal feet (a
5-1/2" h. Rose Bowl was
also made). **$115-140;
$90-115**

Citron Green #5968, 6" Flower Arranger; #526, 5-1/2" h. Large Rose Bowl, Tiffin Optic. **$45-70 each**

Desert Red #500, 6-1/4" h. Rose Bowl, Tiffin Optic, c. 1965. **$65-90**

Chapter 38

Corning Museum of Glass: Tiffin Glass Collection

Twenty pieces of Tiffin Glass were placed in the Corning Museum of Glass in Corning, New York, as a permanent loan in 1992 by the Tiffin Glass Collectors Club. A selection of various shapes from the 1920s through the 1960s were included in the donation. Items donated were: #6727 Crystal Vase; #6590 Ruby and Crystal Empress Ash Tray; #17350 Copen Blue Vase, sand carved Roses; #6317 Crystal Vase; #5942 Crystal Handled Urn Vase; #92 Twilight Vase; Cobalt Blue and Crystal Rose Bowl, unknown line number; #17430 Killarney Sweet Pea Vase; #27 Desert Red Bowl; #16273 Black Satin Aster Vase; #16255 Black Satin Poppy Vase; #310 Sky Blue Satin Fan Vase; #41-26 Crystal Sandwich Glass Dessert Plate; #7240 Sierra, Crystal Water Goblet; #7240 Strawberry Diamond and Fan, Crystal Wine Goblet; #15024 Classic, Rose Pink Water Goblet; #17623 Alexandria, Crystal Water Goblet with Gold Encrustation; #17594 Palais Versailles, Crystal Sherbet with Gold Encrustation; #17659 White House, Crystal Water Goblet; and #17395 Crystal Ice Tea Goblet.

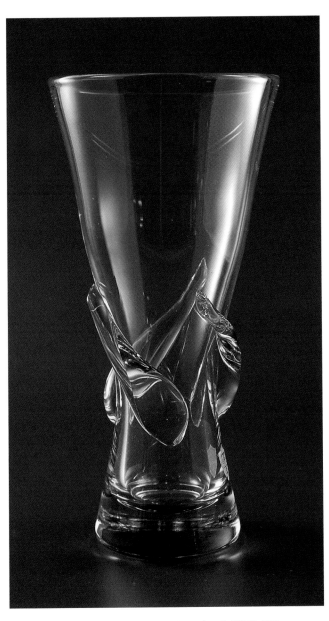

Crystal #6727, 10-3/4" h. Vase, with appliqué. **$150-200**

Copen Blue #17350, 12-3/4" h. Flared Vase, sand carved Roses, Swedish Optic. **$175-225**

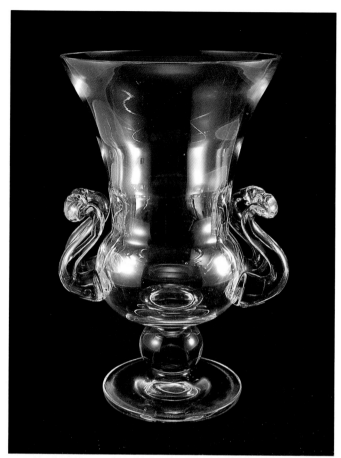

Ruby and Crystal #6590, 11" Ash Tray, 10 Rib Optic, Empress Line. **$150-200**

Opposite:

Top left: Crystal #6317, 8" h. Vase, offhand 3-ball foot, Swedish Optic, c. 1940. **$100-125**

Top right: Crystal #5942, 11" h. Handled Urn Vase, Swedish Optic. **$225-275**

Bottom left: Twilight #92, 9-1/4" h. Vases, c. 1953. **$150-175 each**

Bottom right: Cobalt Blue, 8-1/2" h. Rose Bowl (left), Crystal stem and foot, unknown line number, c. 1961. **$175-225**

Sources

In addition to private archival documents, information for this book was taken from the following sources:

Bickenheuser, Fred; *Tiffin Glassmasters, Book III.* (reprinted catalog pages). Grove City, Ohio: Glassmasters Publications, 1985.

Crockery and Glass Journal.

Tiffin Glass Collectors Club. *Tiffin Glassmasters* newsletters and slides.

Tiffin Glass Company. Catalogs: 1967, 1968; "Tiffin Modern" Catalog, 1965.

U.S. Glass Company. Catalogs: 1940, c. 1952, 1955, 1956, 1959, 1960, 1962, "Tiffin Selections" Catalog, 1961.

Tiffin Glass Collectors Club

The Tiffin Glass Collectors Club is a non-profit corporation with tax exempt status, which was established in 1985 to study the history of Tiffin Glass, known as Factory R of the United States Glass Company, and the glassware manufactured there.

Membership in the club includes collectors from all over the United States. A club newsletter is published quarterly for members and features meeting minutes, glass articles, historical data, and other information of interest to collectors.

Activities of the Tiffin Glass Collectors Club include the glass shows held in June and November and fund-raisers which benefit the Archive Foundation and a future Tiffin Glass Museum.

For more information, inquiries may be directed to the Tiffin Glass Collectors Club, P.O. Box 554, Tiffin, Ohio 44883.